Alfred Sisley:

170 Paintings and Drawings

By Narim Bender

****

I0477254

Alfred Sisley: 170 Paintings and Drawings

Paintings&Drawings, Volume 16
Narim Bender
Published by Icon-m, 2014.

Foreword

Alfred Sisley was French impressionist landscape painter, born in Paris to English parents. He was a founding member of the Impressionist group.

Alfred Sisley received an excellent education, even studying English and business in London before returning to Paris in 1862. He took the opportunity to study the works of John Constable and William Turner. However Sisley wasn't attracted to the business-world and returned to Paris at age 23. His father supported him and decided to send him to the École des Beaux-Arts in the atelier of Charles-Gabriel Gleyre. Fellow students of Gleyre included Pierre-Auguste Renoir, Claude Monet and Frédéric Bazille. Their friendship was to revolutionize painting and radically change the history of art. Together they would paint landscapes in the open air in order to realistically capture transient effects of sunlight. This innovative approach resulted in paintings more colorful and more broadly painted than the public was accustomed to seeing. Consequently, Sisley and his friends initially had few opportunities to exhibit or sell their work.

Sisley's student works are lost. His earliest known work, Lane near a Small Town, is believed to have been painted around 1864. His first landscape paintings are sombre, coloured with dark browns, greens, and pale blues. They were often executed at Marly and Saint-Cloud..

After 1871, Sisley lived modestly at Moret-sur-Loing and painted subtly shimmering small-town landscapes that reveal a wistful, lyrical sensibility. Influenced by his friends Renoir and Monet in his selection of colours, Sisley was less daring than Monet in his use of the "rainbow palette" and closer to the Barbizon School tradition.

Among the Impressionists Sisley has been overshadowed by Monet, although his work most resembles that of Camille Pissarro. Described by art historian Robert Rosenblum as having "almost a generic character, an impersonal textbook idea of a perfect Impressionist painting", his work strongly invokes atmosphere, and his skies are always impressive. He concentrated on landscape more consistently than any other Impressionist painter.

He never deviated into figure painting and, unlike Renoir and Pissarro, never found that Impressionism did not fulfill his artistic needs.

Among Sisley's best-known works are Street in Moret and Sand Heaps, both owned by the Art Institute of Chicago, and The Bridge at Moret-sur-Loing, shown at Musée d'Orsay, Paris.

Sisley produced some 900 oil paintings, some 100 pastels and many other drawings, although he only lived to be 59 years old. The canvases Sisley painted in his later life were not always of the quality and invention of his paintings of the 1870's and 80's, as he seemed to become constrained by a preoccupation with technique. Unlike Monet or Renoir he did not confront urban life in his landscapes, and his view of nature was not shaped by anarchist politics like Pissarro's. Instead he painted a timeless yet unsentimental view of nature in which man, although present, is never the controlling force. Sisley eventually achieved a considerable reputation but it was won at a high price and he had little time to enjoy it. Sisley died in Moret-sur-Loing on January 29, 1899 of throat cancer, just a few months after the death of his wife.

Drawings

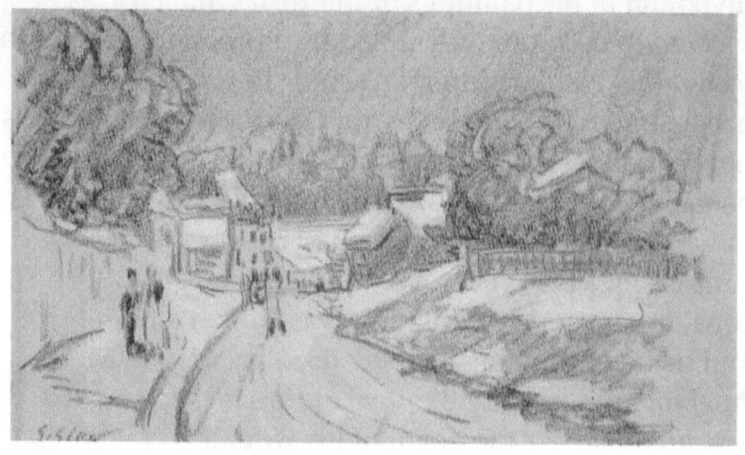

Early Snow at Louveciennes
1871-1872, pastel

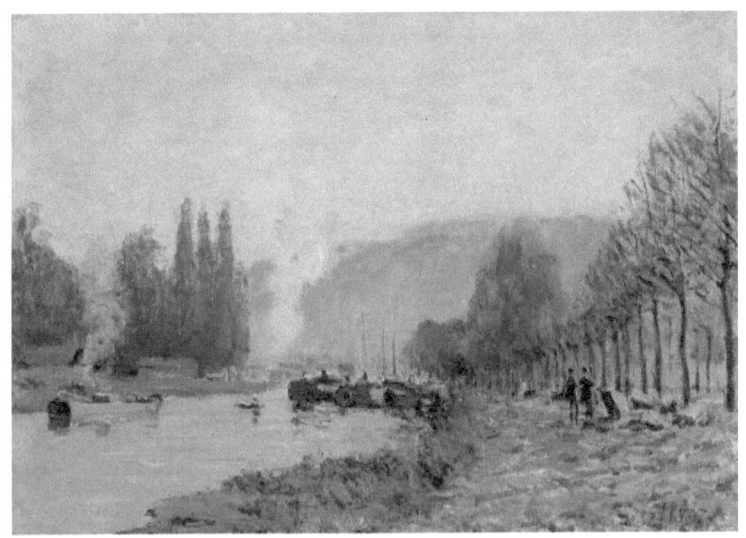

The Seine at Bougival
1873, chalk

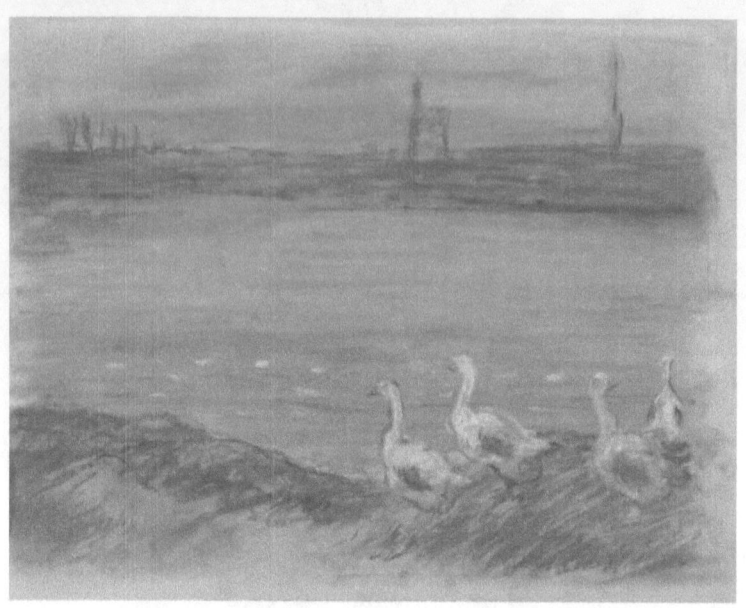

Four Geese by a Pond
1875, Pastel on heavy cream paper

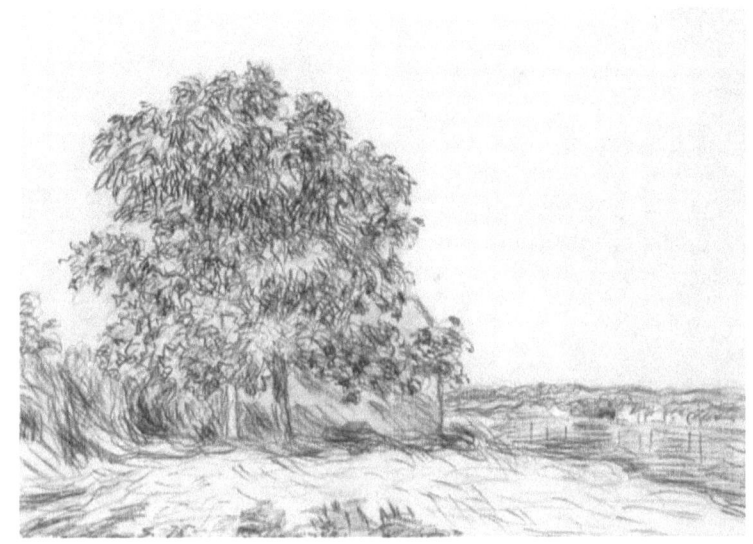

Plain Thomery and village of Champagne
1876, black and white chalk on paper

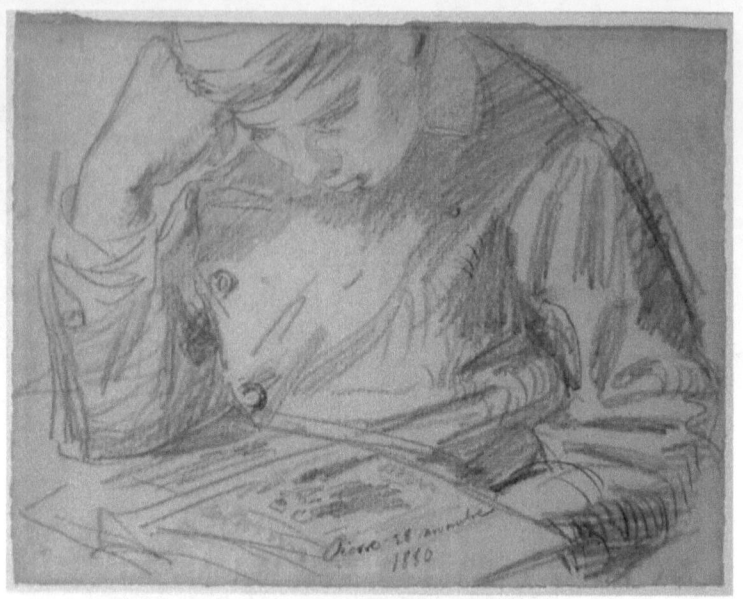

The Artist's Son, Pierre
1880, pencil

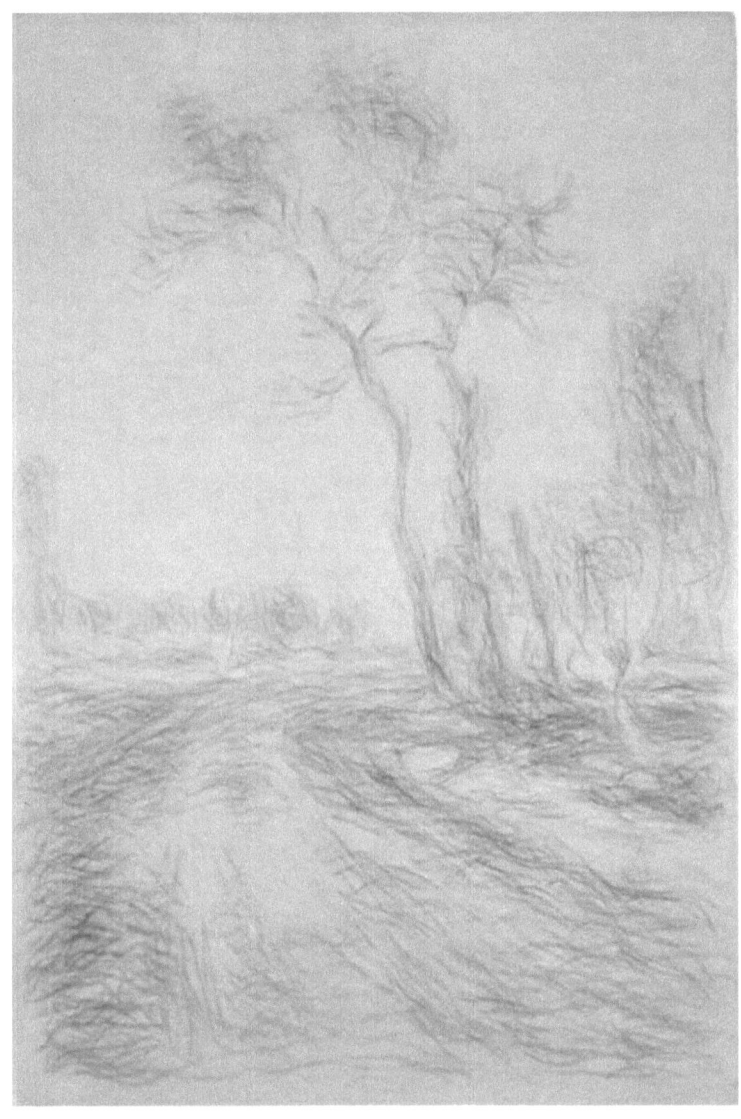

Landscape with Trees
1880-85, Pastel and colored pencils on tan laminated
card

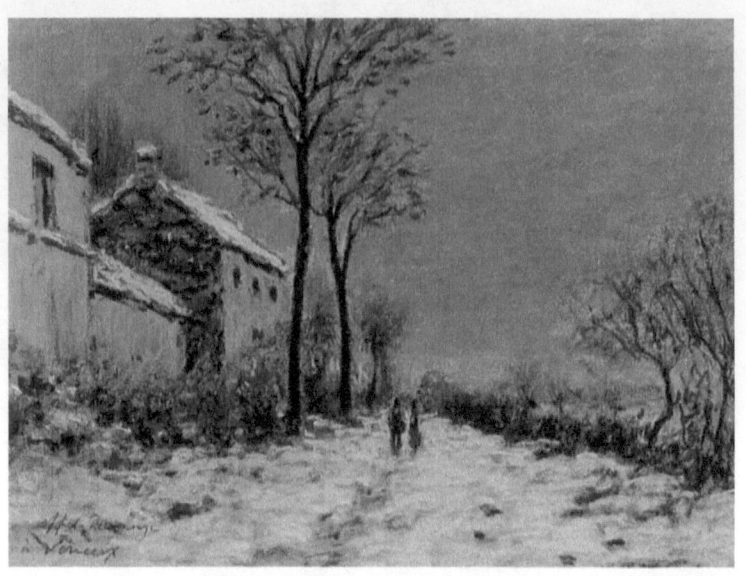

The Effect of Snow at Veneux
1884, pastel

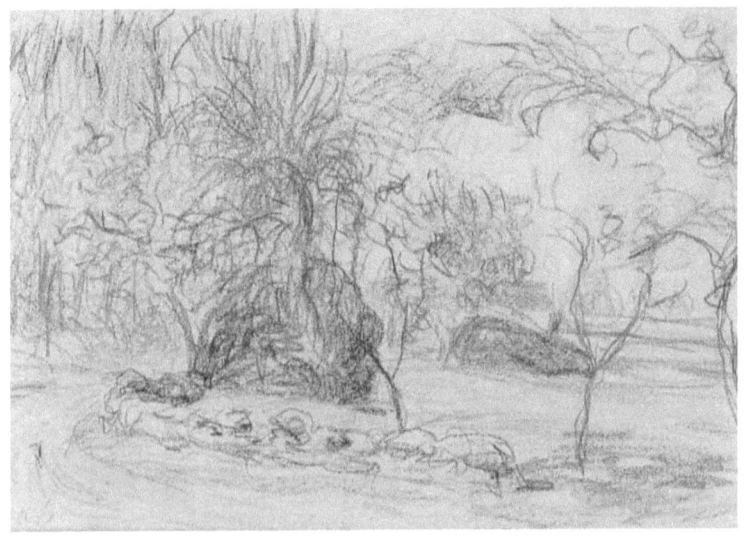

Orchard
1885, pastel

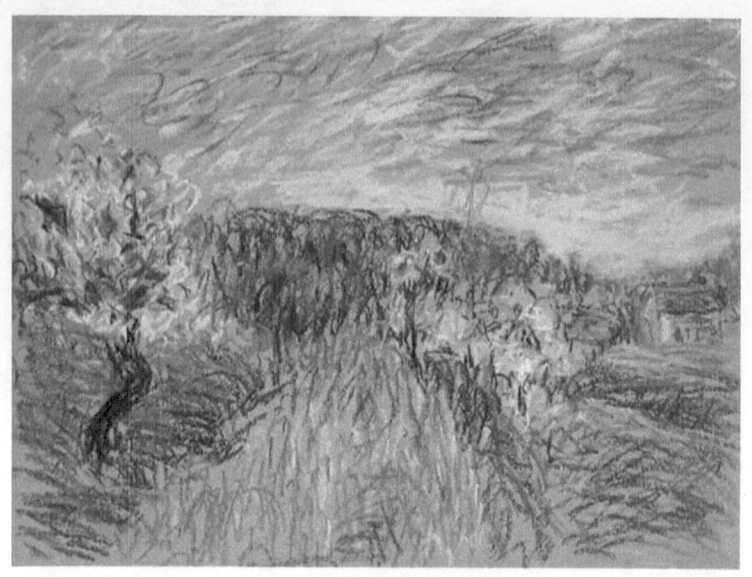

Two isolated houses
1886, pastel

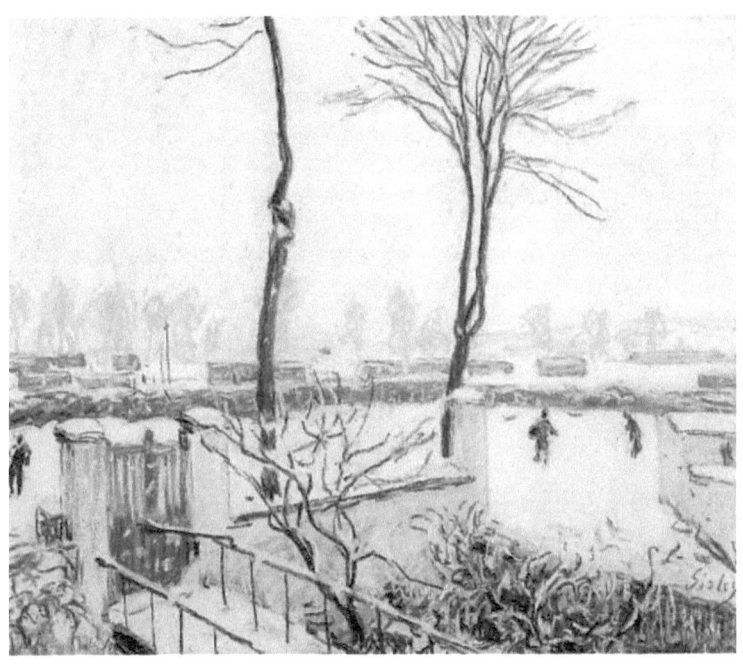

Approach to the Railway Station
1888, pastel

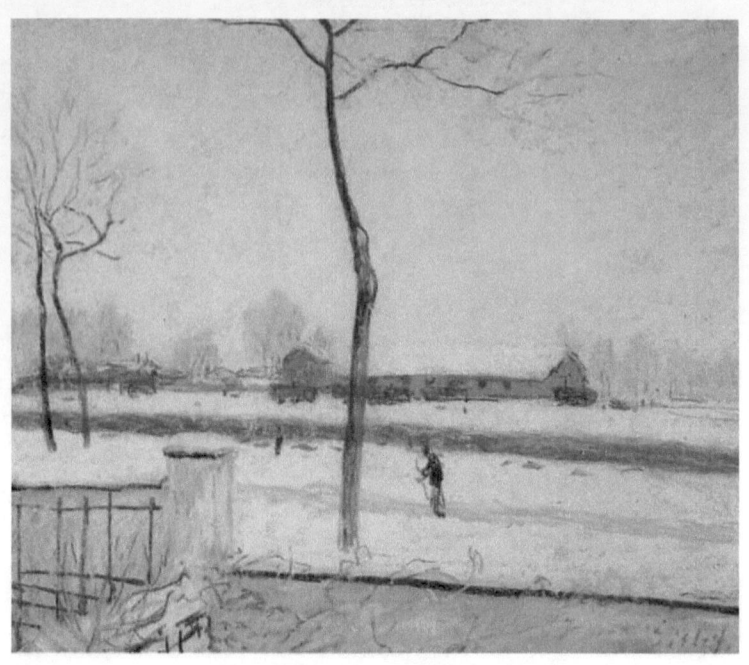

Snow Scene - Moret Station
1888, pastel

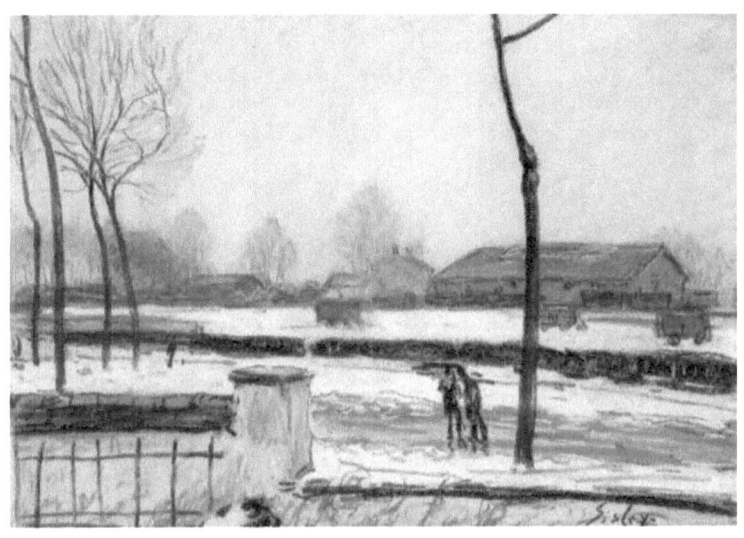

Winter Landscape, Moret
1888, pastel

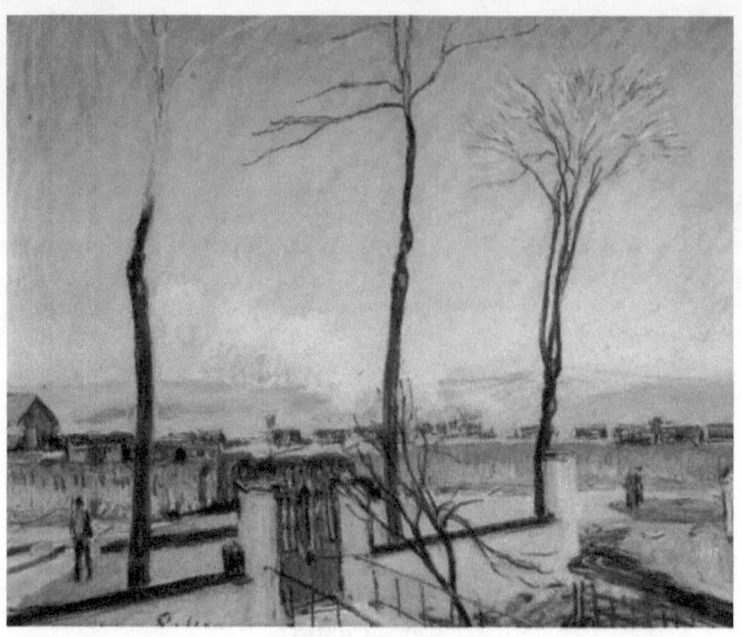

Winter Sun, Moret
1888, pastel

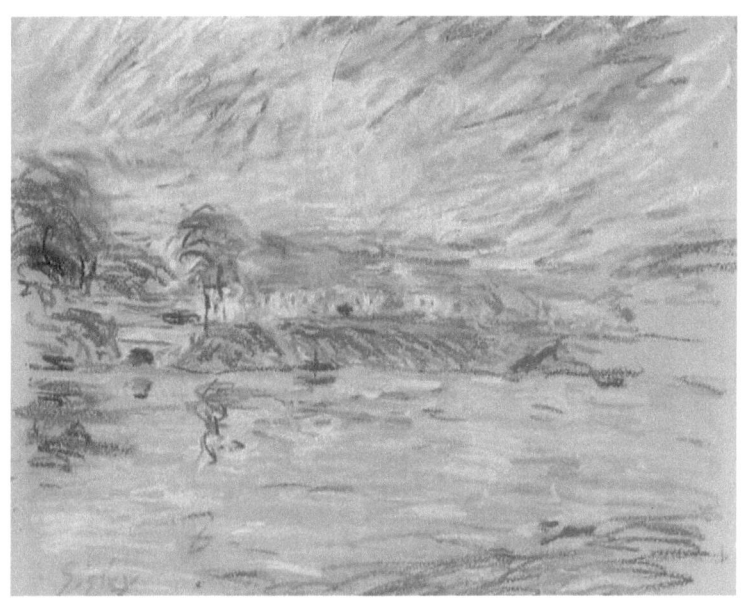

View of a Village by a River
1888-1892, pastel

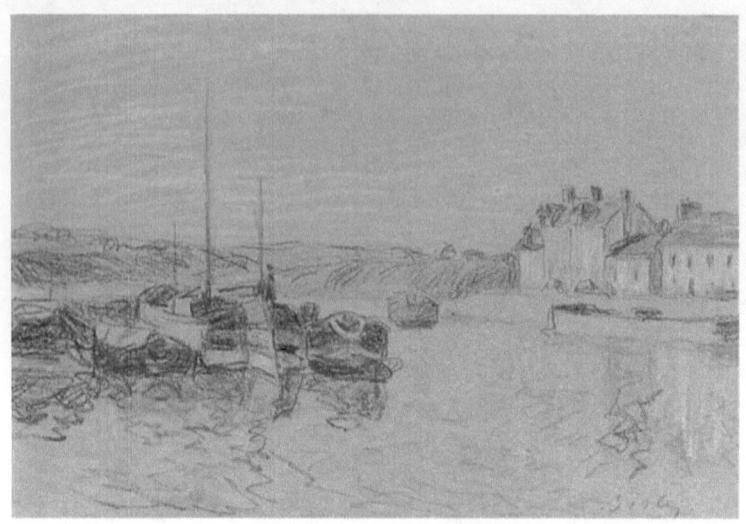

Le canal du Loing à Saint Mammès
1888, pastel on paper

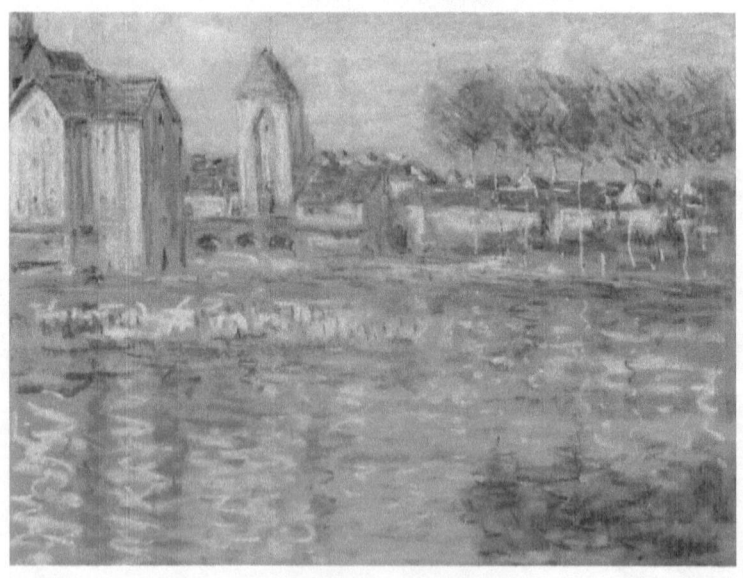

Moret-sur-Loing
1888-1892, pastel

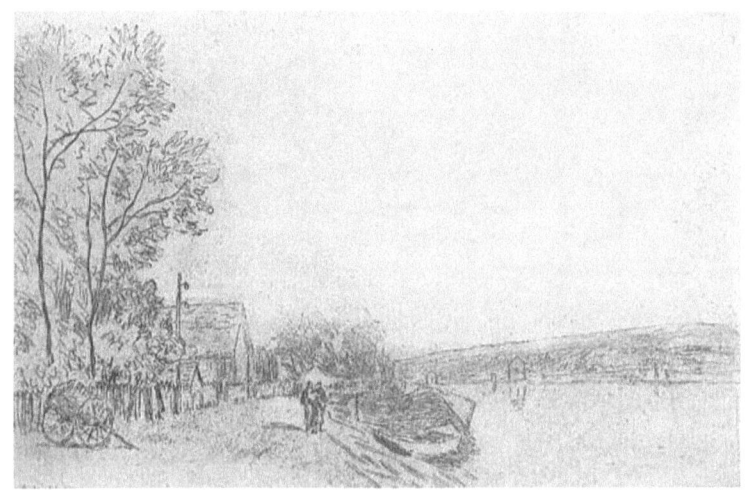

Banks of the Loing, the cart
1890, etching

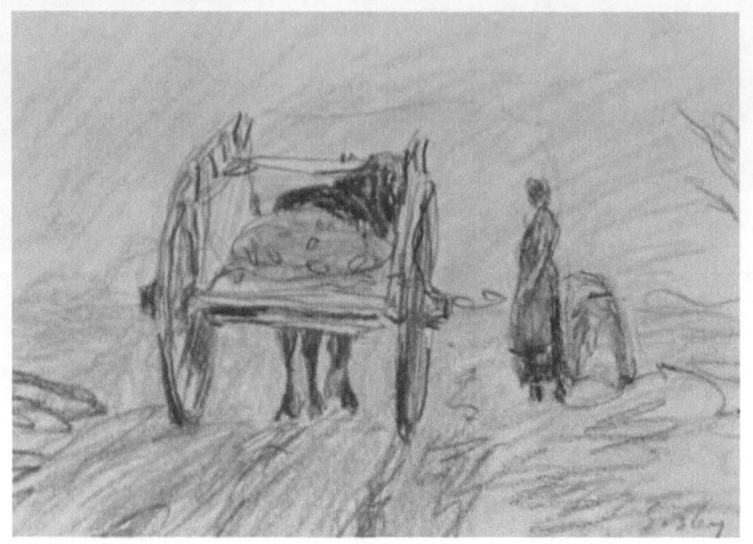

Cart and farmer
1890-1895, color pencil on paper

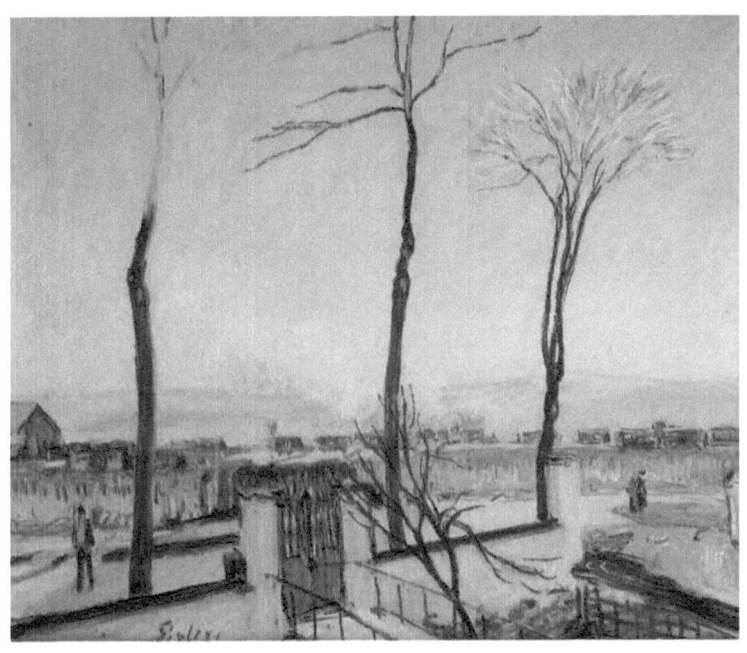

Snow Effect at Moret
1894, pastel

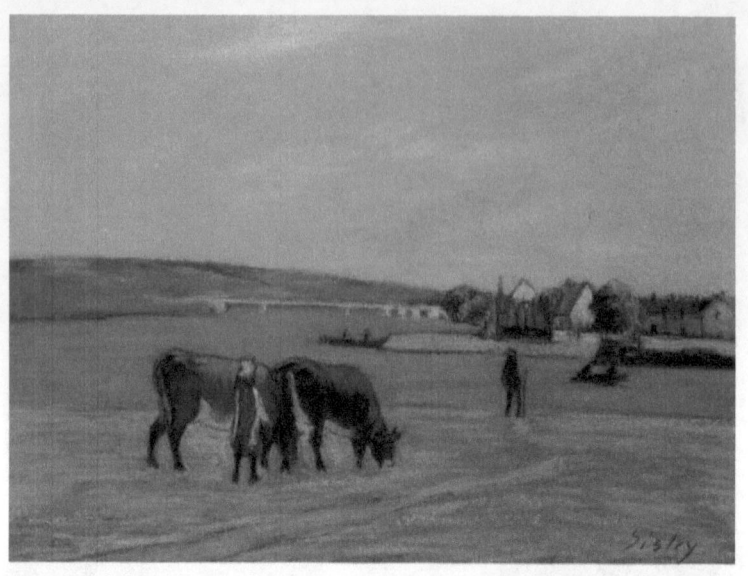

Cows by the Seine at Saint-Mammes
1895, pastel

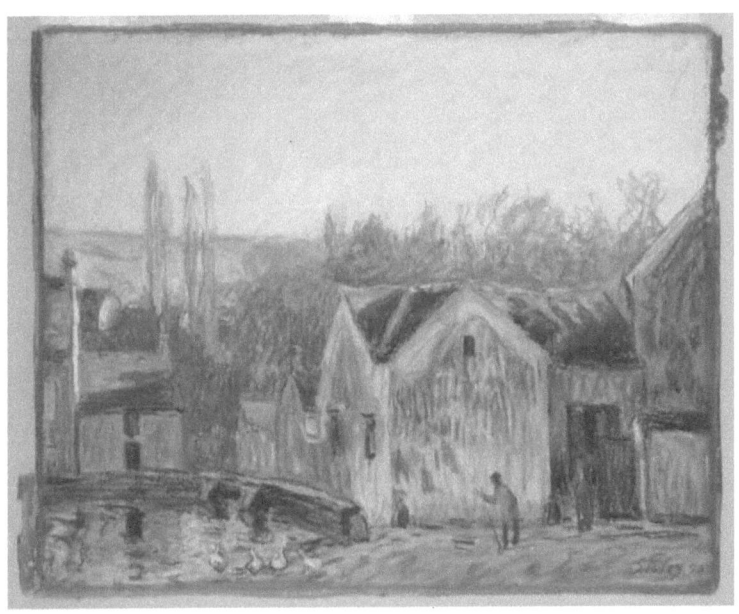

A Corner of Moret-sur-Loing
1895, Pastel, with stumping, on gray wove paper with
blue fibers (discolored to tan)

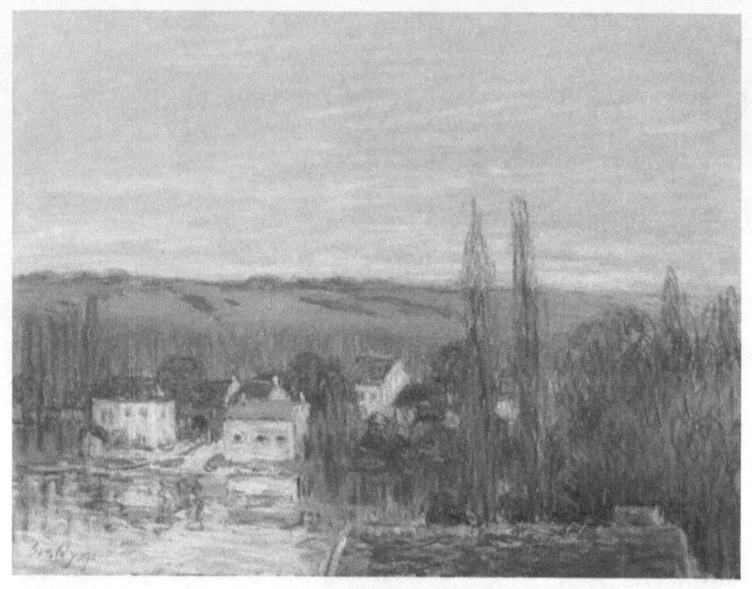

Trough of Marly
1895, pastel on oatmeal paper

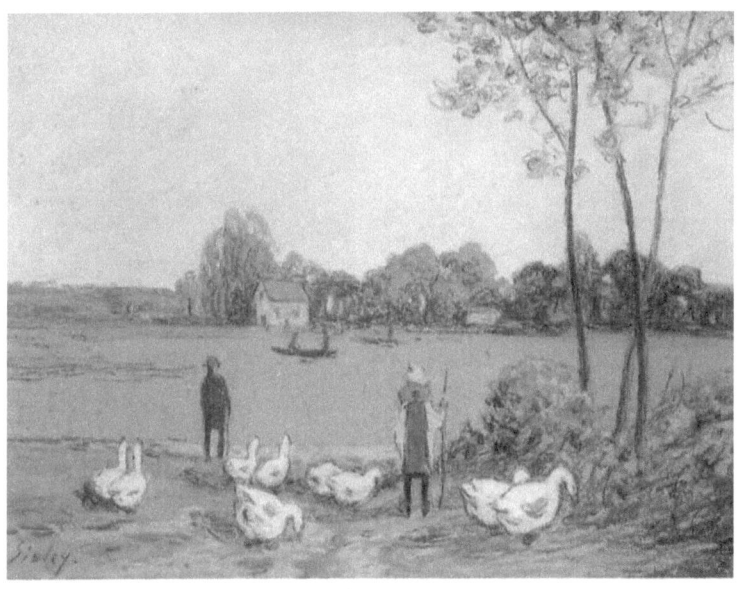

By the River Loing
1896, pastel

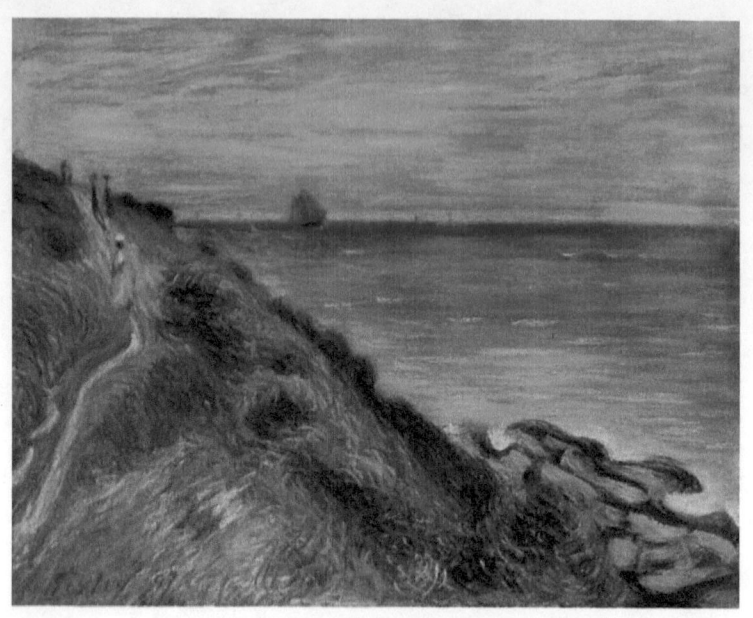

On the Cliffs, Langland Bay, Wales
1897, pastel

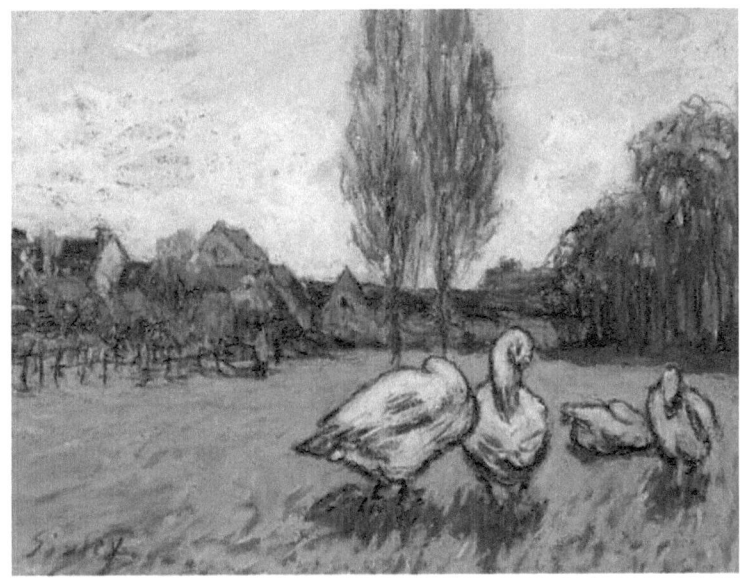

Geese
1897, pastel

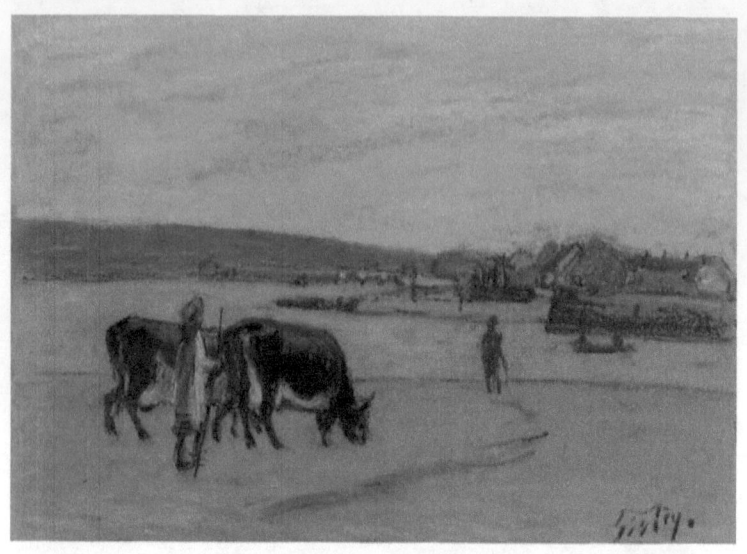

Pasture by the Seine
1897, pastel

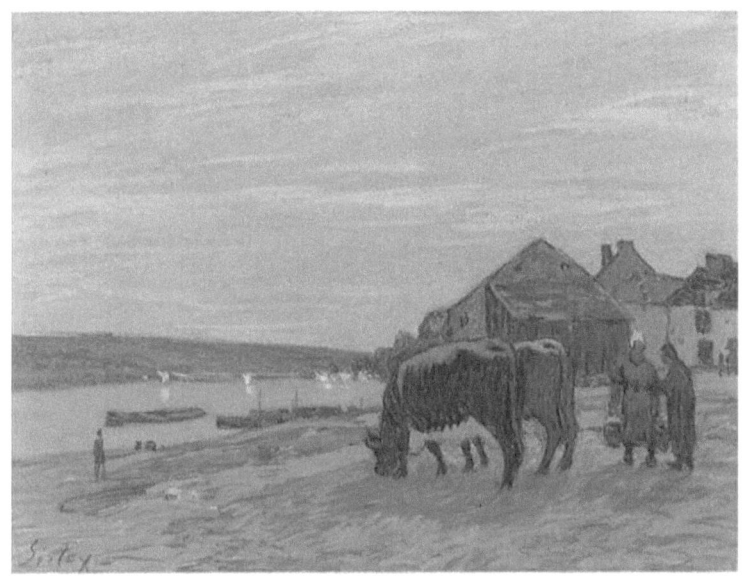

Cows at pasture
1897, pastel

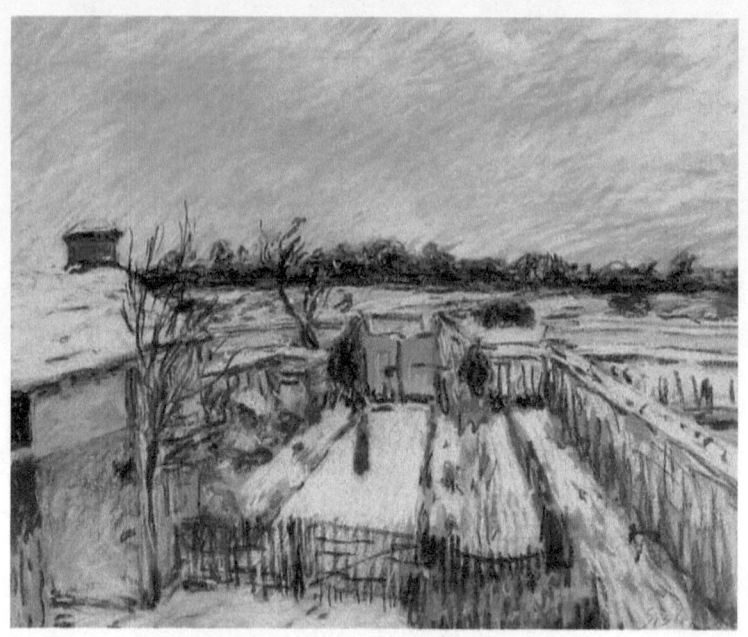

The Garden under the Snow
N.d., pastel

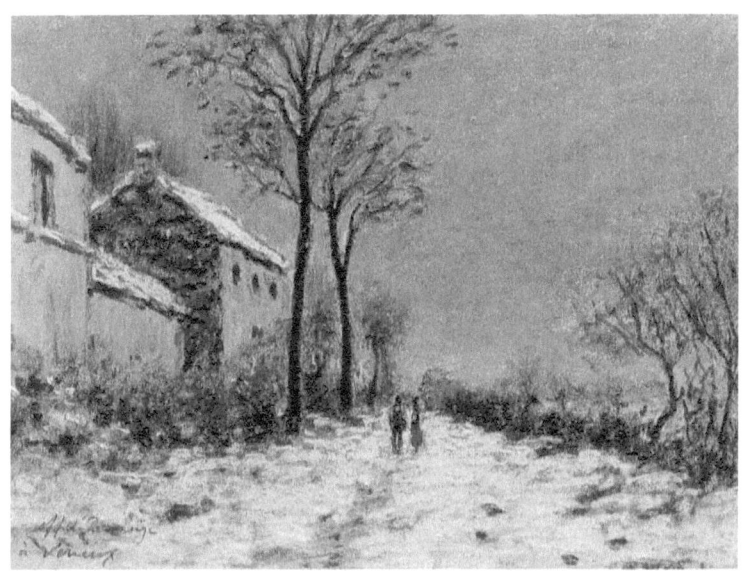

Snow Effect at Veneux
N.d., pastel

Narim Bender

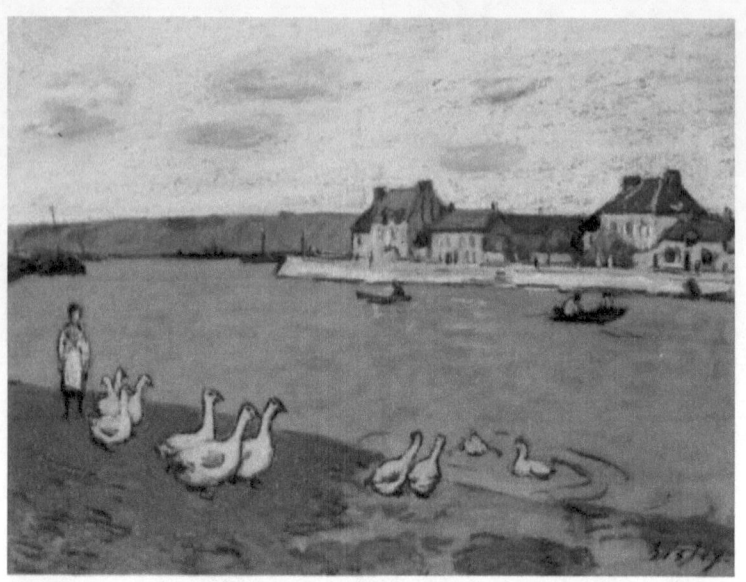

Geese along the Loing River
N.d., pastel

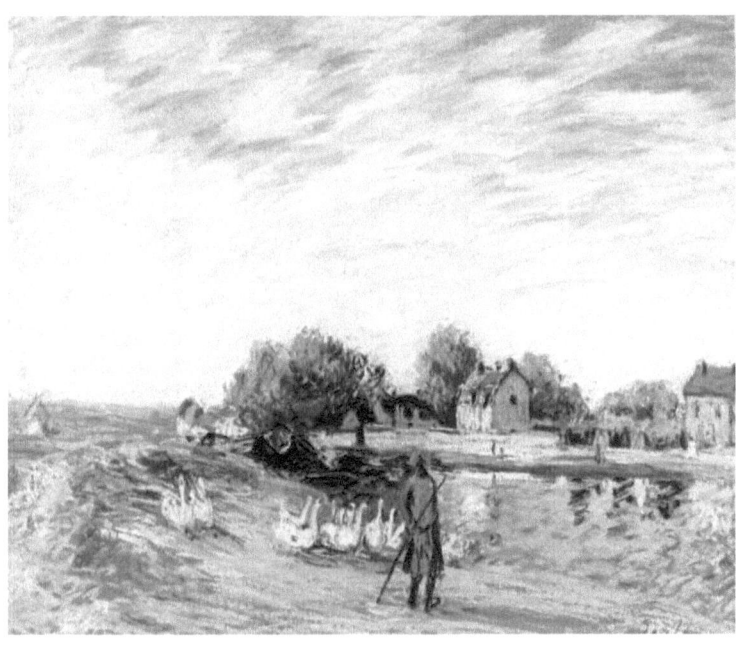

Geese at Saint-Mammes
N.d., pastel

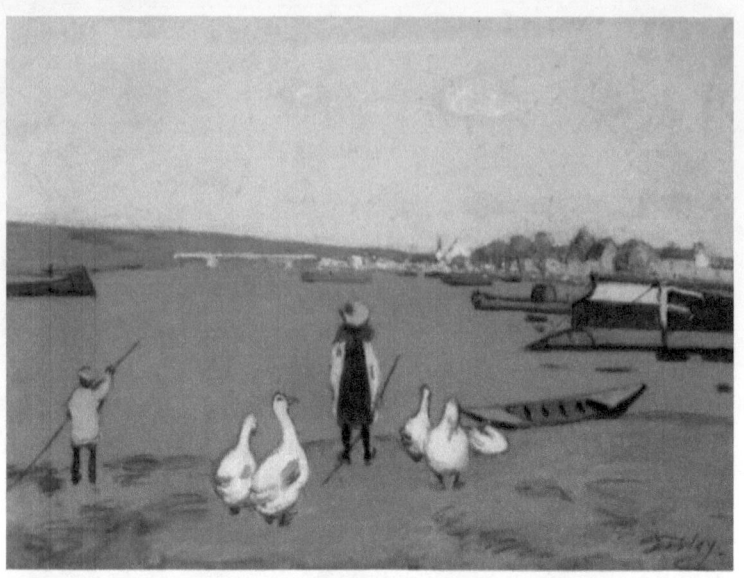

Goose Keeper along the Loing River
N.d., pastel

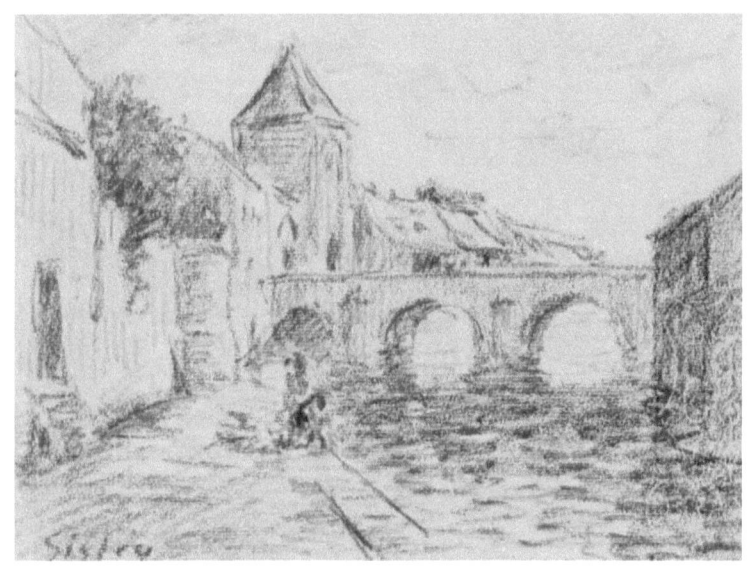

View of Moret-sur-Loing
N.d., pastel

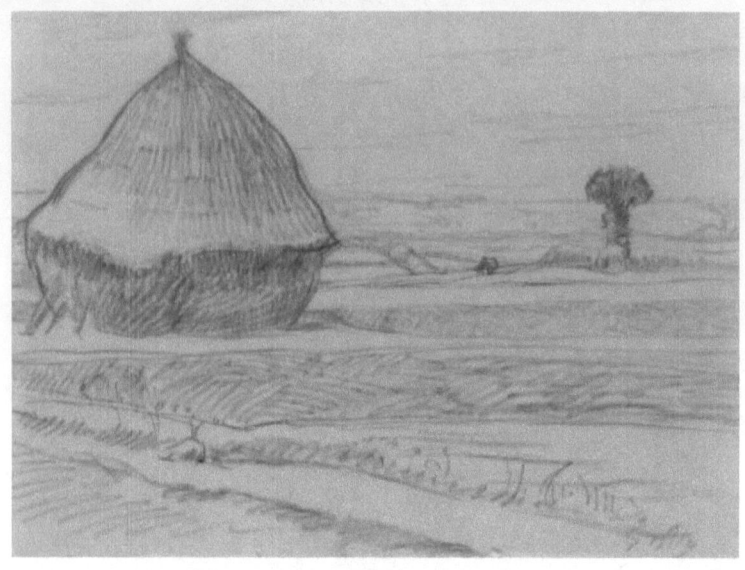

Haystacks
N.d., black Conté crayon on buff paper

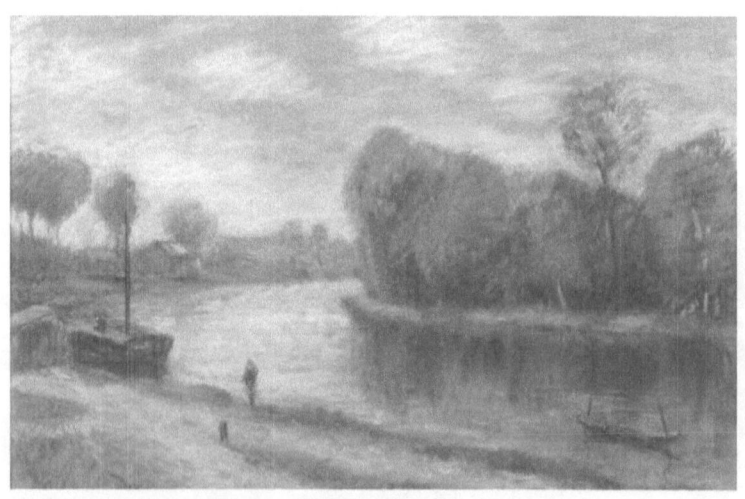

Riverside
N.d., pastel

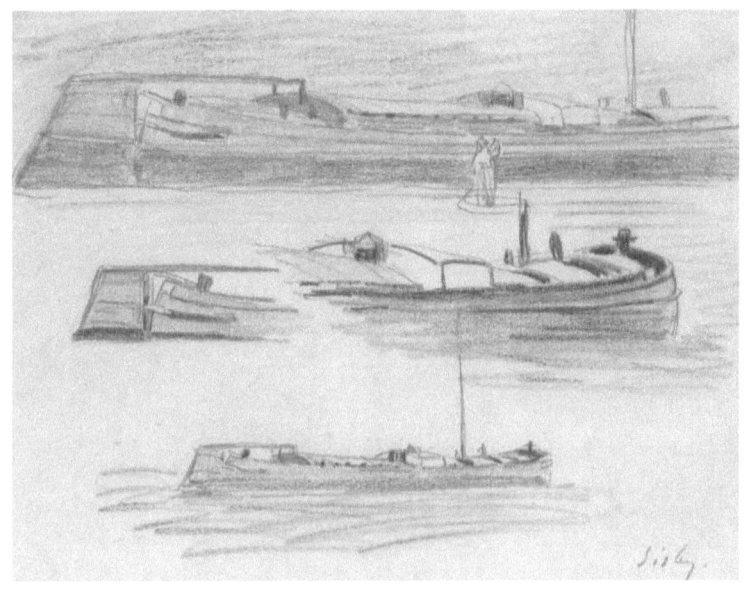

Barges
N.d., wax crayon and pencil on paper

This drawing was executed on the banks of the Seine near the Ile de la Grande Jatte, as the statue depicted seems to be the now famous Statue of Liberty executed by Bartholdi which was installed there shortly after the large version in New York Harbour.

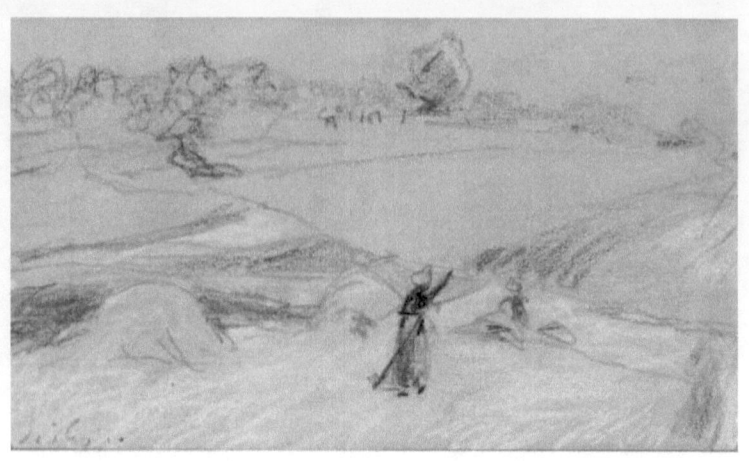

Landscape
N.d., Pastel and pencil on paper

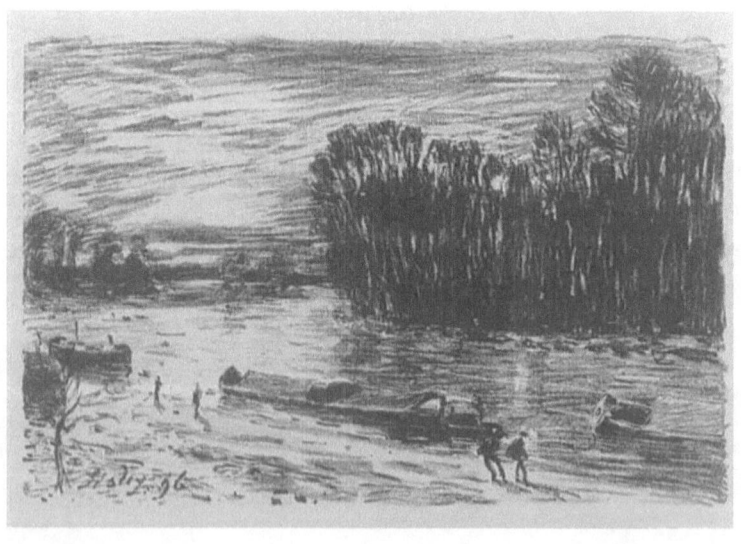

Edge of Loing, Near St Mammes
N.d., Litograph

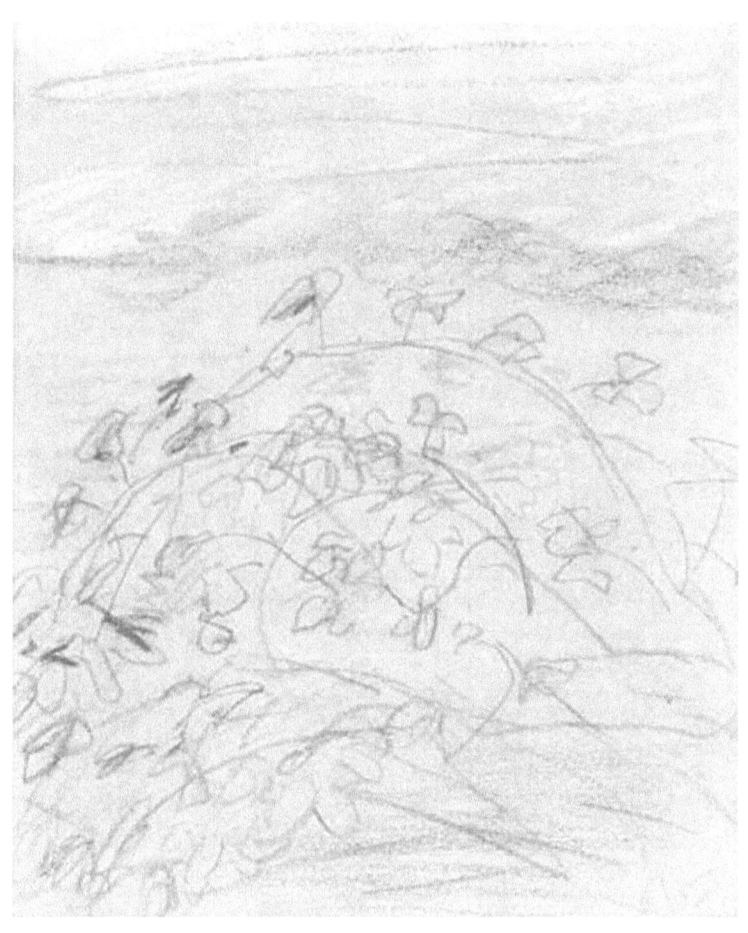

Bush
N.d., Pastel on paper

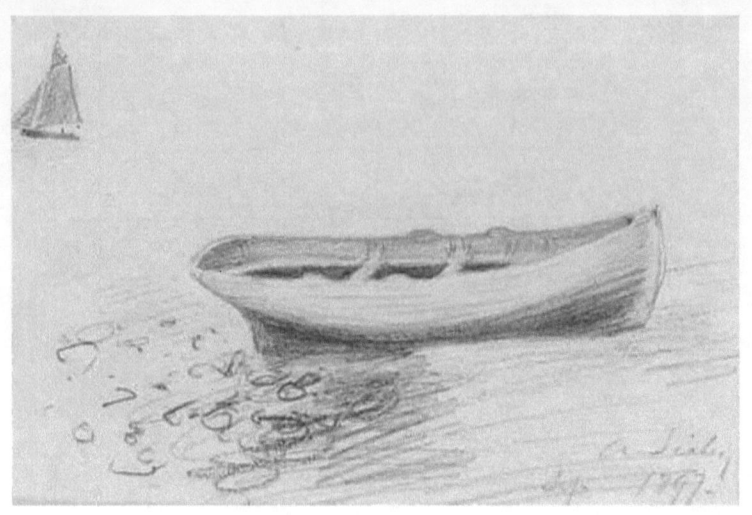

Study of boats
N.d., pencil on paper

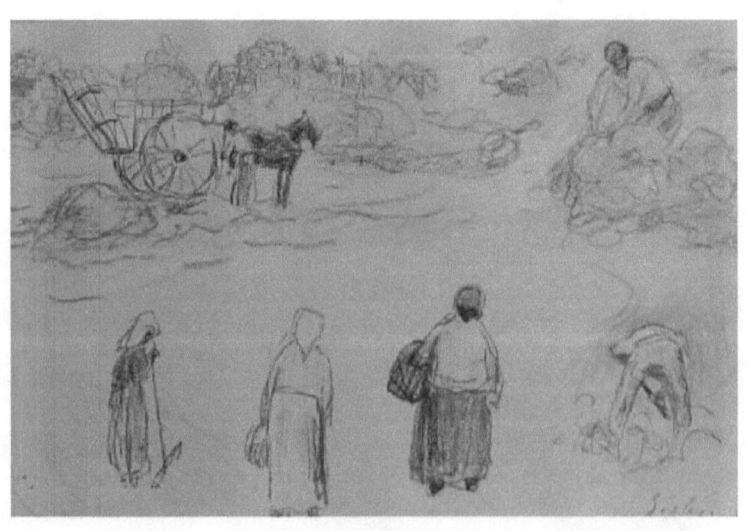

Studies of characters at work
N.d., wax crayon

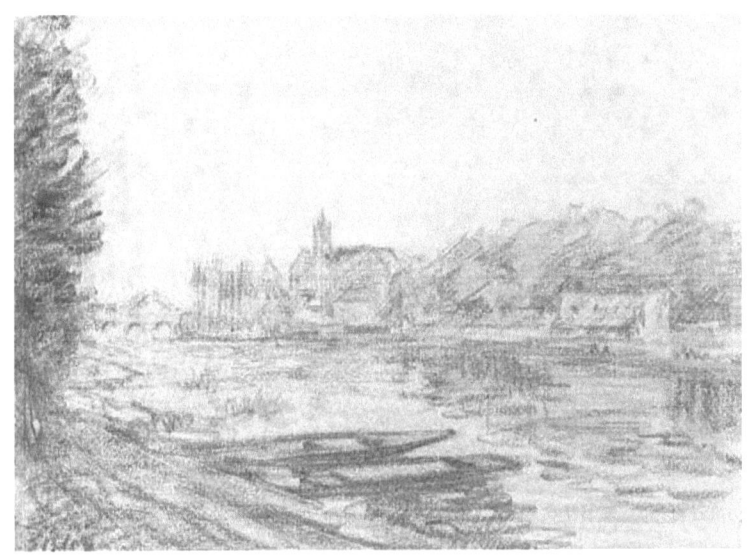

The banks of the Loing
N.d., Pastel on paper

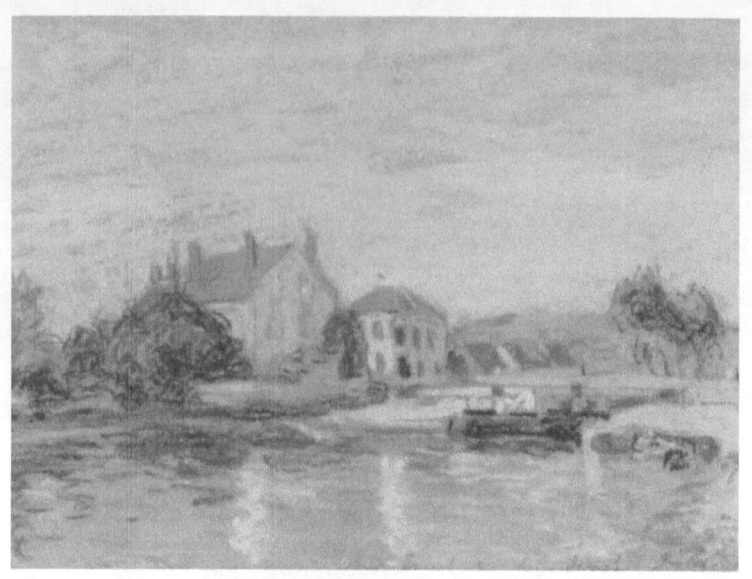

Homes at the Edge
N.d., Pastel on paper

Paintings

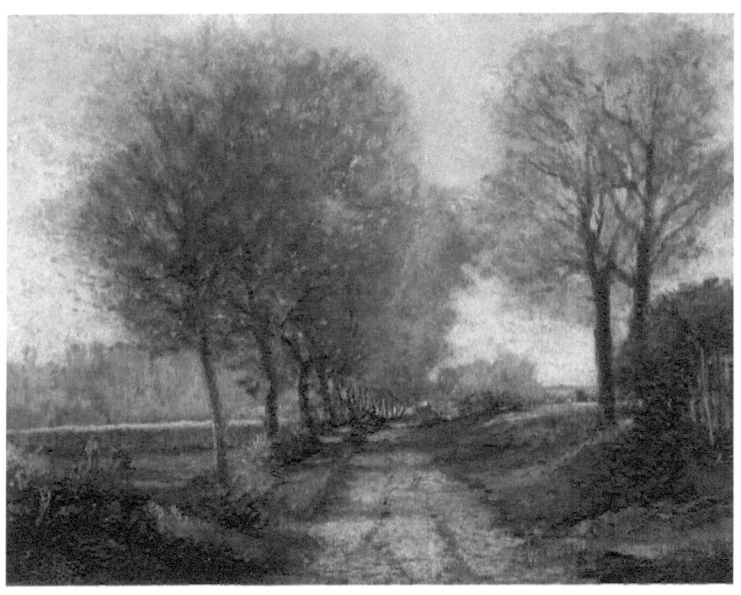

Lane near a Small Town
1864, oil on canvas

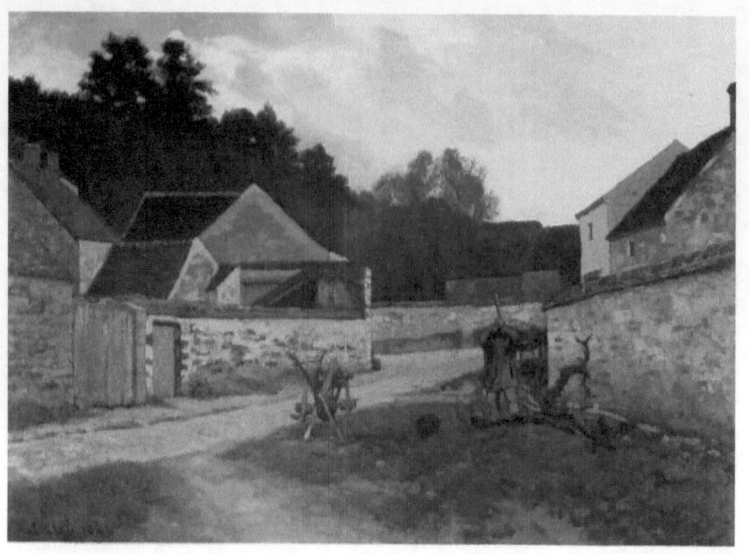

Village Street in Marlotte
1866, oil on canvas

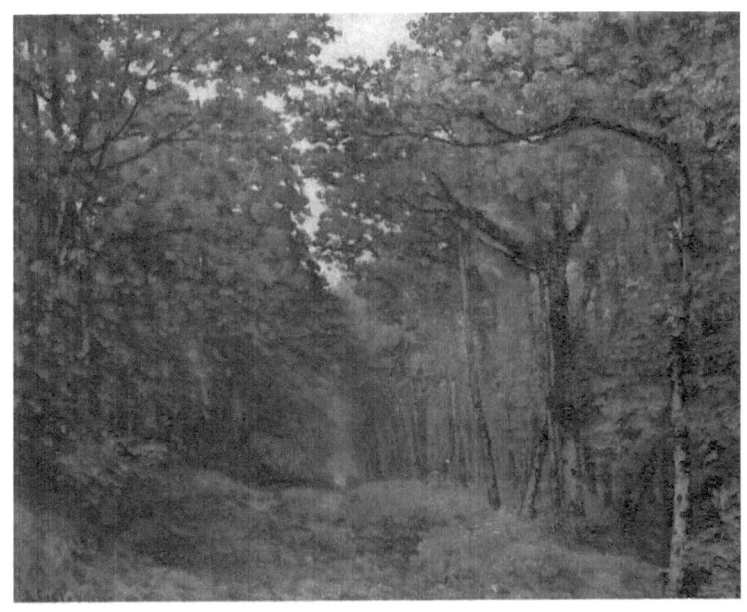

Avenue of Chestnut Trees near La Celle-Saint-Cloud
1867, oil on canvas

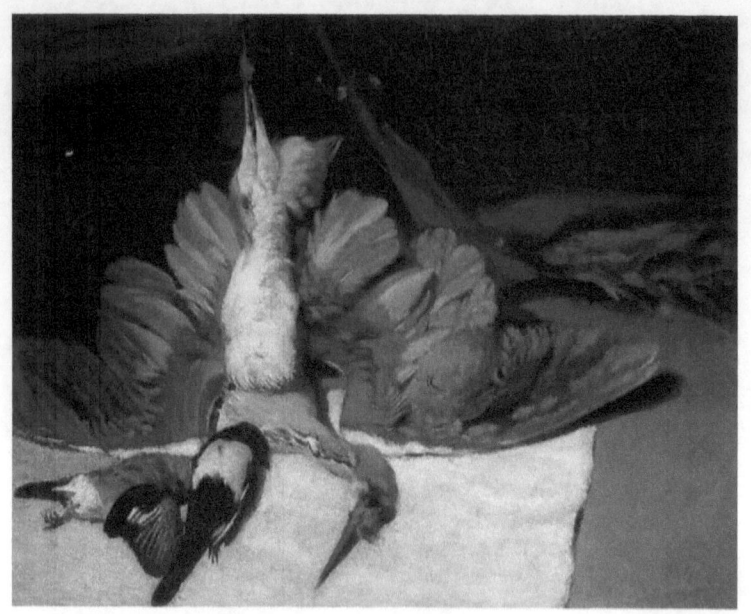

Still Life with Heron
1867, oil on canvas

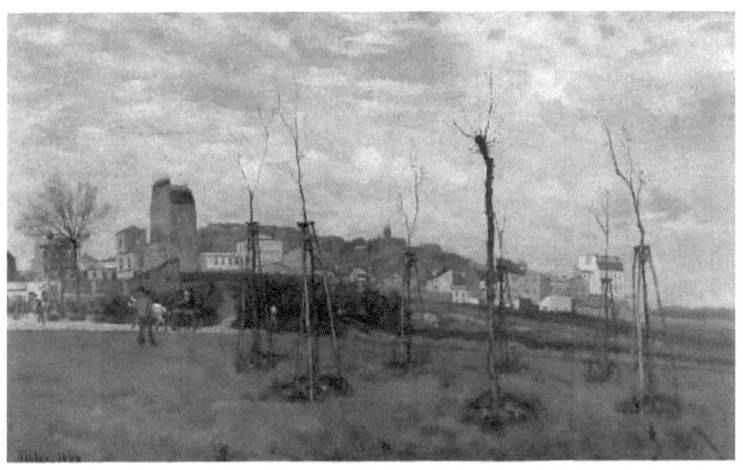

View of Montmartre from the Cite des Fleurs, Les
Batignolles
1869, oil on canvas

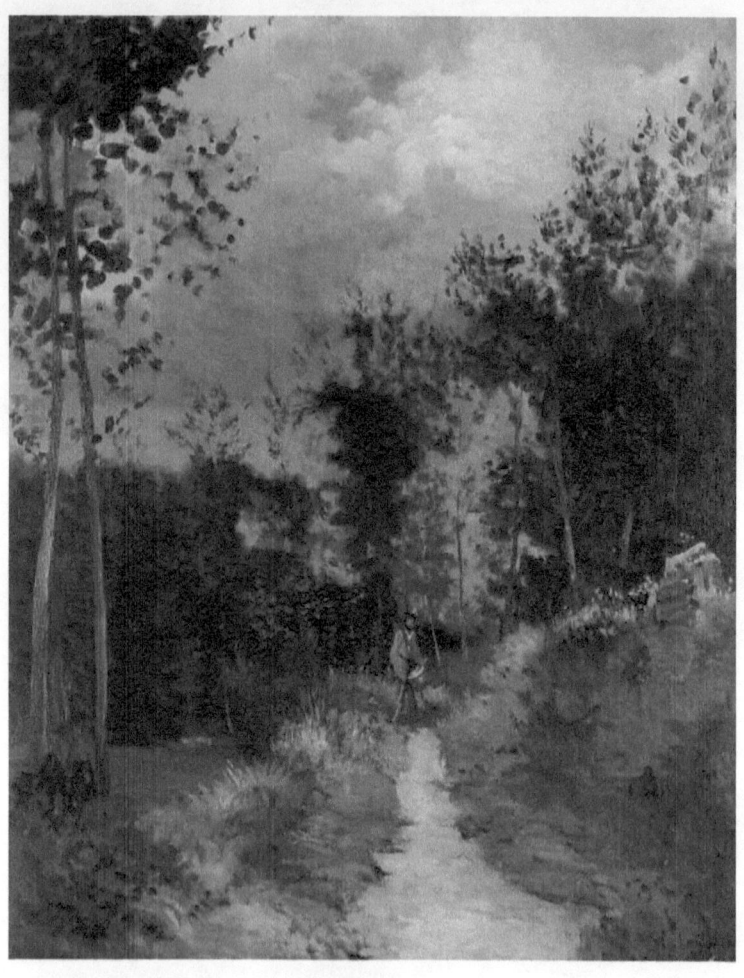

Rural Guardsman in the Fountainbleau Forest
1870, oil on canvas

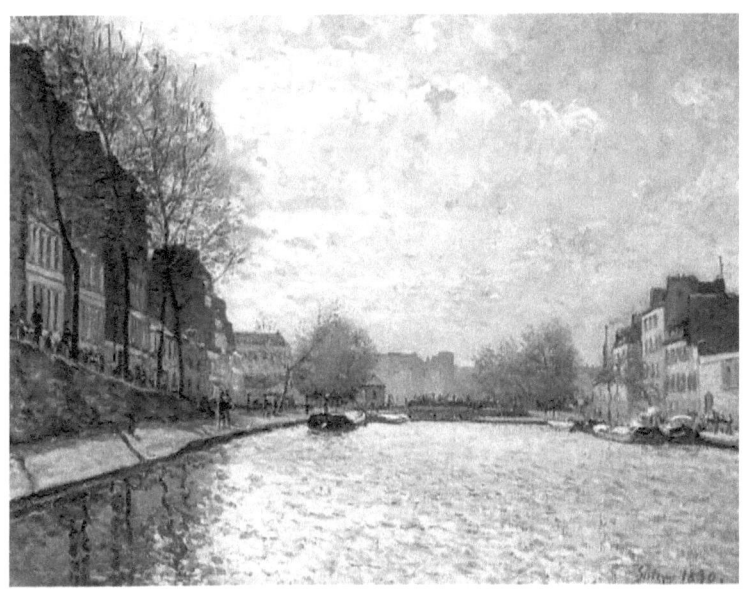

View of the Canal St. Martin
1870, oil on canvas

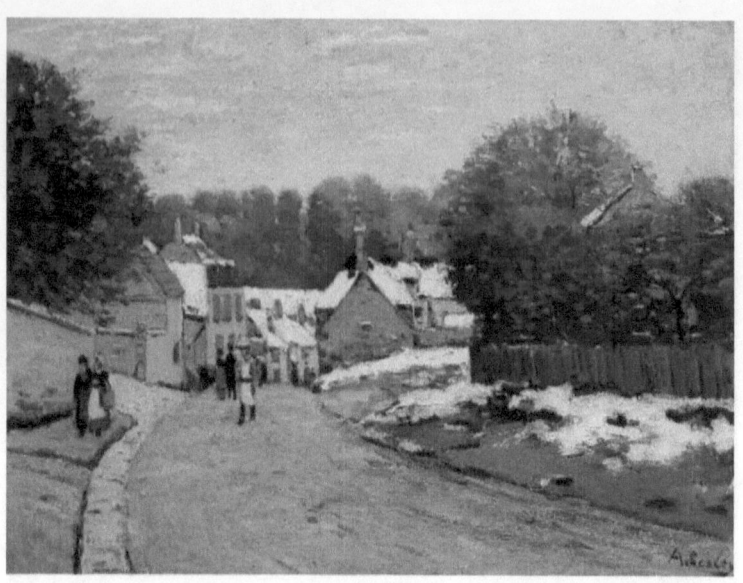

Early Snow at Louveciennes (also known as Rue de Voisins, Louveciennes: First Snow) 1871-72, oil on canvas

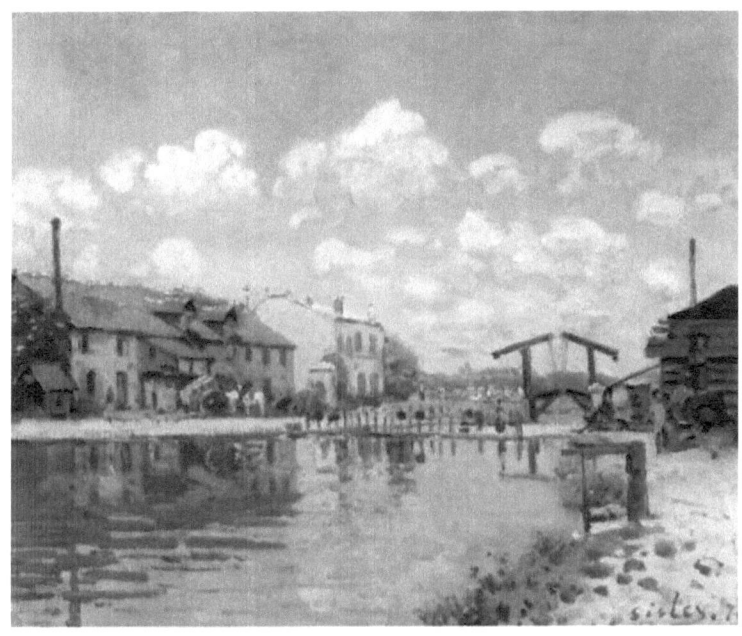

The Saint-Martin Canal
1872, Oil on canvas,

Sisley's work around 1870 showed his interest in the colour impressions of trees and buildings and particularly in the shifting play of light and cloud on a landscape. He painted the waters of the Seine at Bougival or Marly as sensitively as the nuances of snow colour in Pissarro's beloved lanes and gardens of Louveciennes.

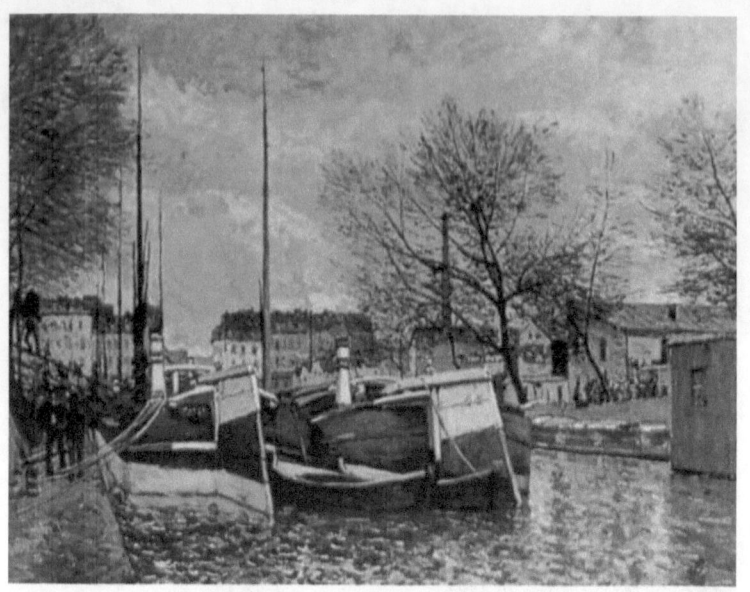

Barges on the Saint-Martin Canal
1872, oil on canvas

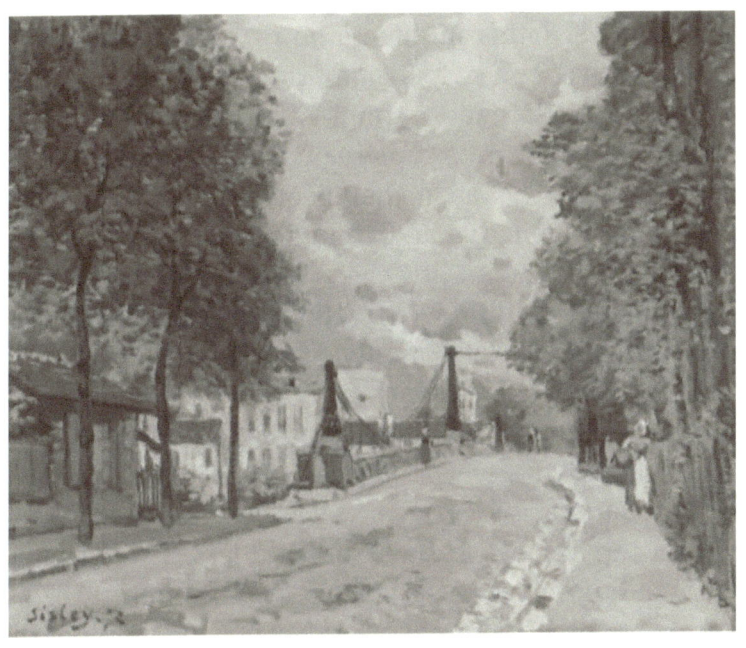

The road to Gennevilliers
1872, oil on canvas

Painted in 1872, this sunlit summer scene depicts the stone and cast-iron suspension bridge that leads into Villeneuve-la-Garenne, a small village on the left bank of the Seine a few miles upstream from Sisley's home at Louveciennes. The bridge had been opened in 1844, connecting Villeneuve-la-Garenne to Saint-Denis on the opposite bank and ending the village's relative isolation. One could now travel north from Paris to Saint-Denis, a distance of only seven kilometers, and then cross the bridge (which rested on the island of Saint-Denis) to reach Villeneuve. The picturesque village quickly became a popular spot for Parisian day trippers and vacationers, as well as serving as a river port for the nearby town of Gennevilliers. Sisley visited this area twice during the spring and summer of 1872, producing a sequence of six landscapes that explore the regional road access to the capital and both the recreational and commercial activities on the banks of the Seine here.

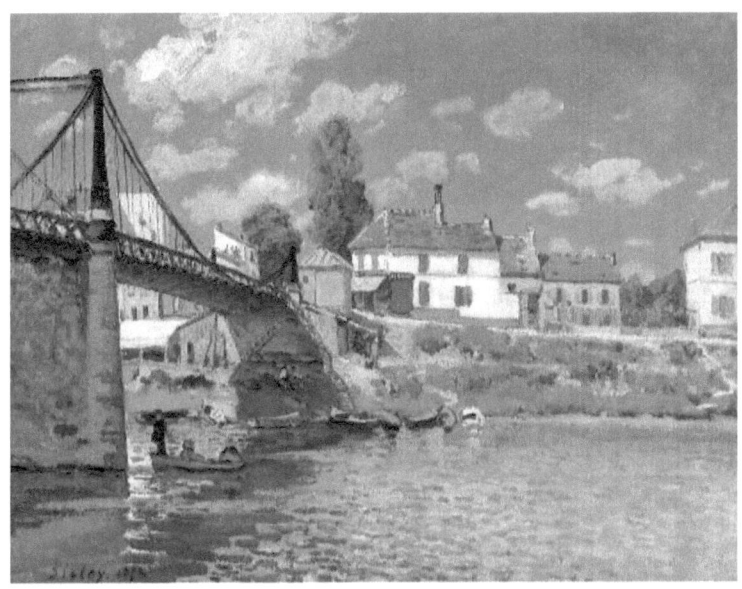

Bridge at Villeneuve-la-Garenne
1872, oil on canvas

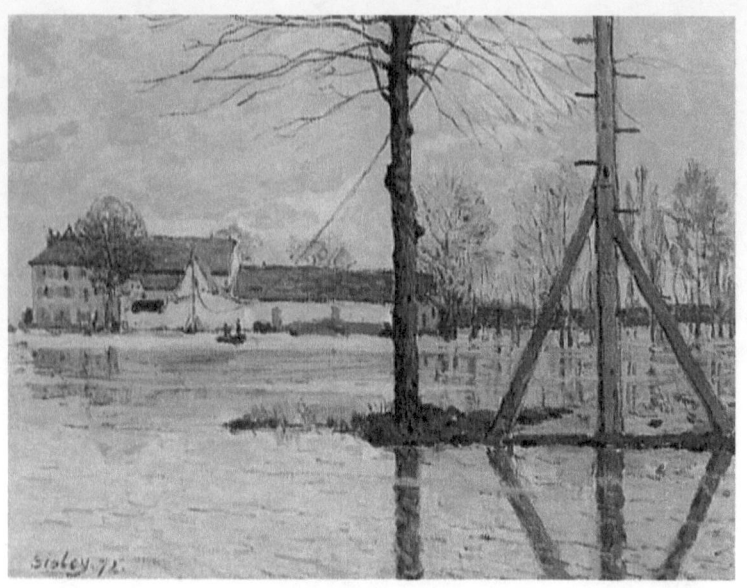

Ferry to the Ile-de-la-Loge, Flood
1872, oil on canvas

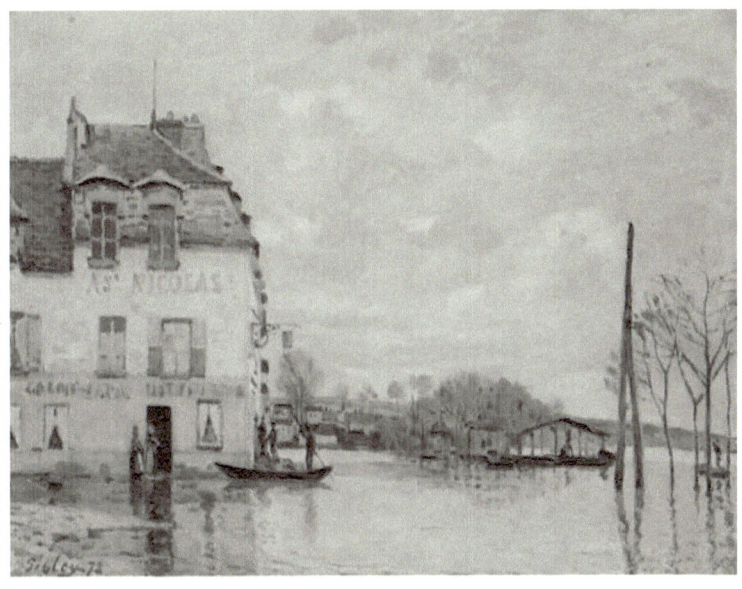

Flood at Port-Marly
1872, oil on canvas

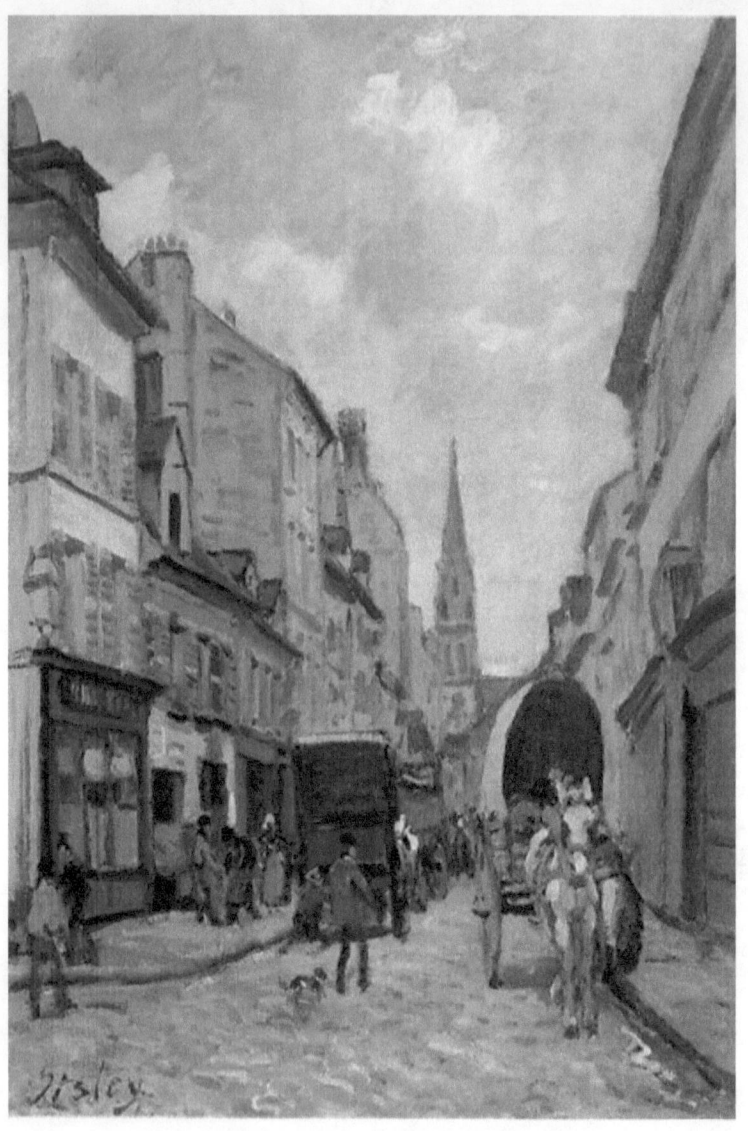

La Grand Rue, Argenteuil
1872, oil on canvas

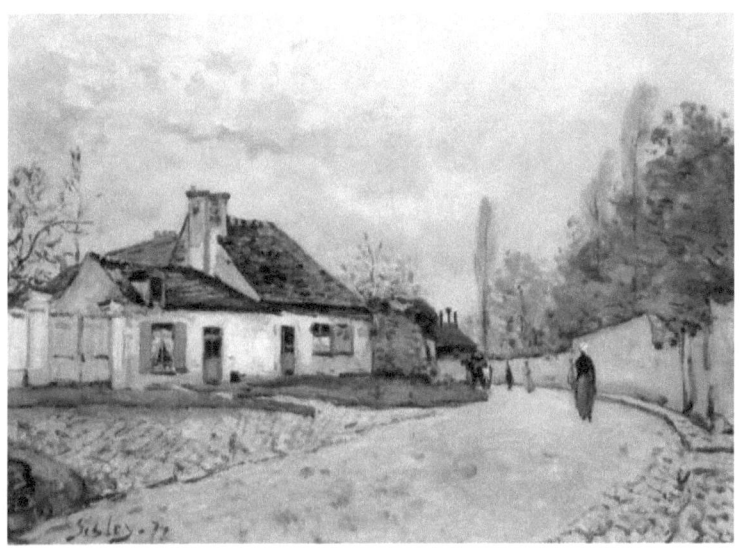

Neighborhood Street in Louveciennes (also known as
Rue de Village (Voisins to Louveciennes)
1872, oil on canvas

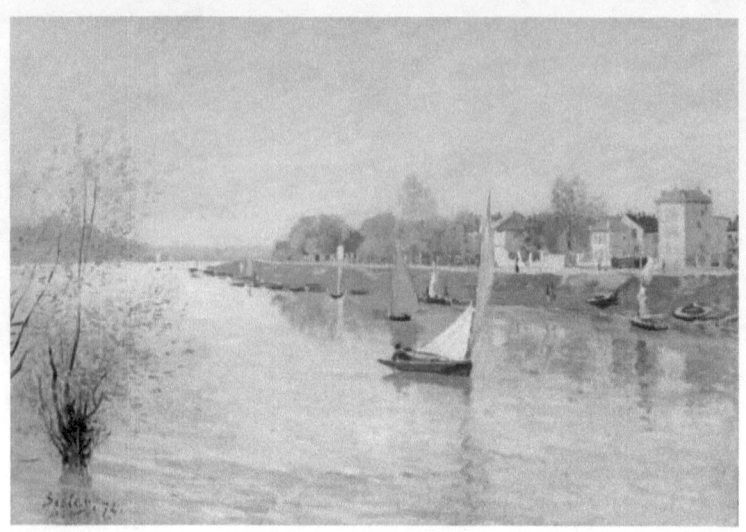

The Seine at Argenteuil
1872, oil on canvas

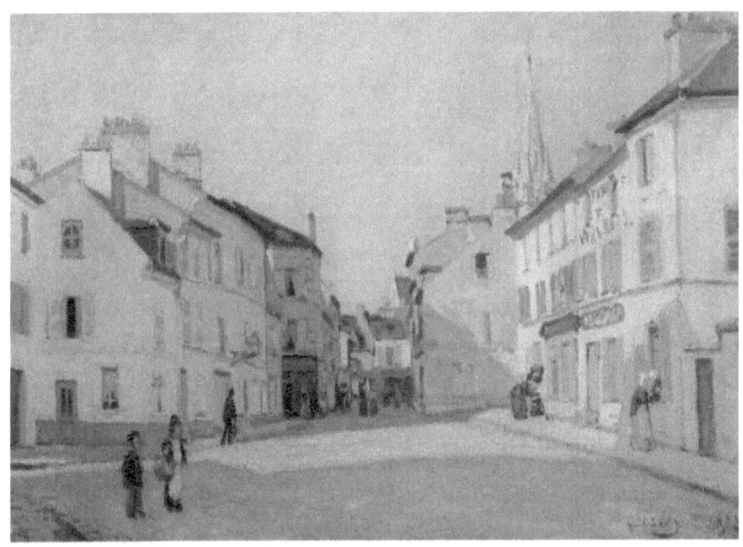

Square in Argenteuil (also known as Rue de la
Chaussee)
1872, oil on canvas

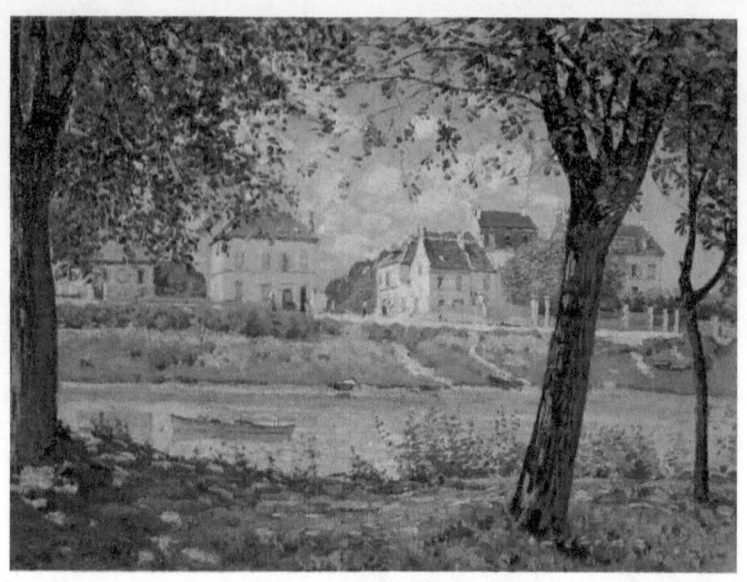

Village on the Banks of the Seine (also known as
Villeneuve-la-Garenne)
1872, oil on canvas

In this painting, created two years before the first
Impressionist exhibition, light already reigns supreme.
It floods the background in defiance of the traditions of
aerial perspective, while the bank closer to the viewer is
shrouded in shadow.

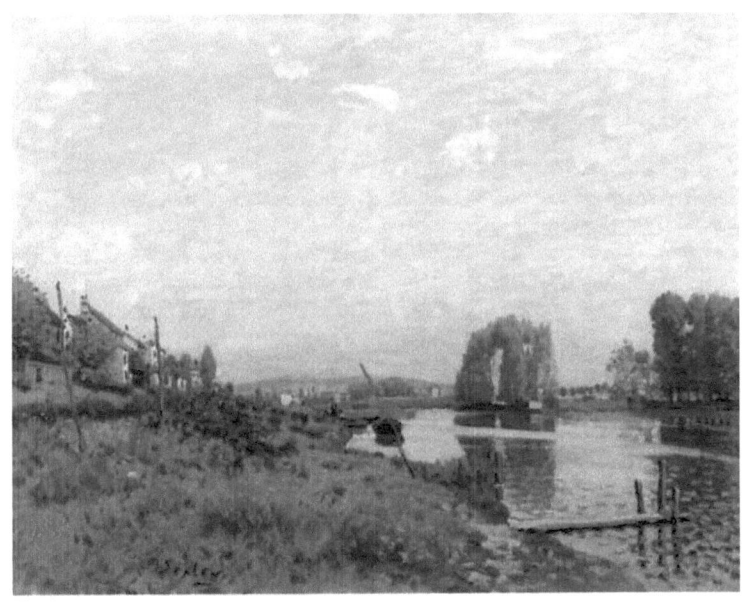

The Island of Saint-Denis
c. 1872, Oil on canvas,

Sisley's work around 1870 showed his interest in the colour impressions of trees and buildings and particularly in the shifting play of light and cloud on a landscape.

In this painting the outline, as used to define the form of an object, is avoided. The material quality is dissolved; nature becomes merely an illusion. The colours of the spectrum define the colour palette; black, for example, is hardly ever used.

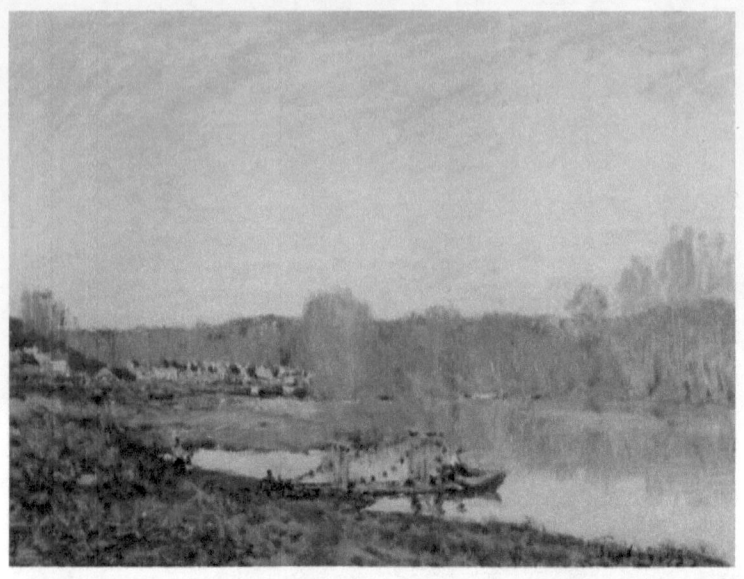

Autumn - Banks of the Seine near Bougival
1873, oil on canvas

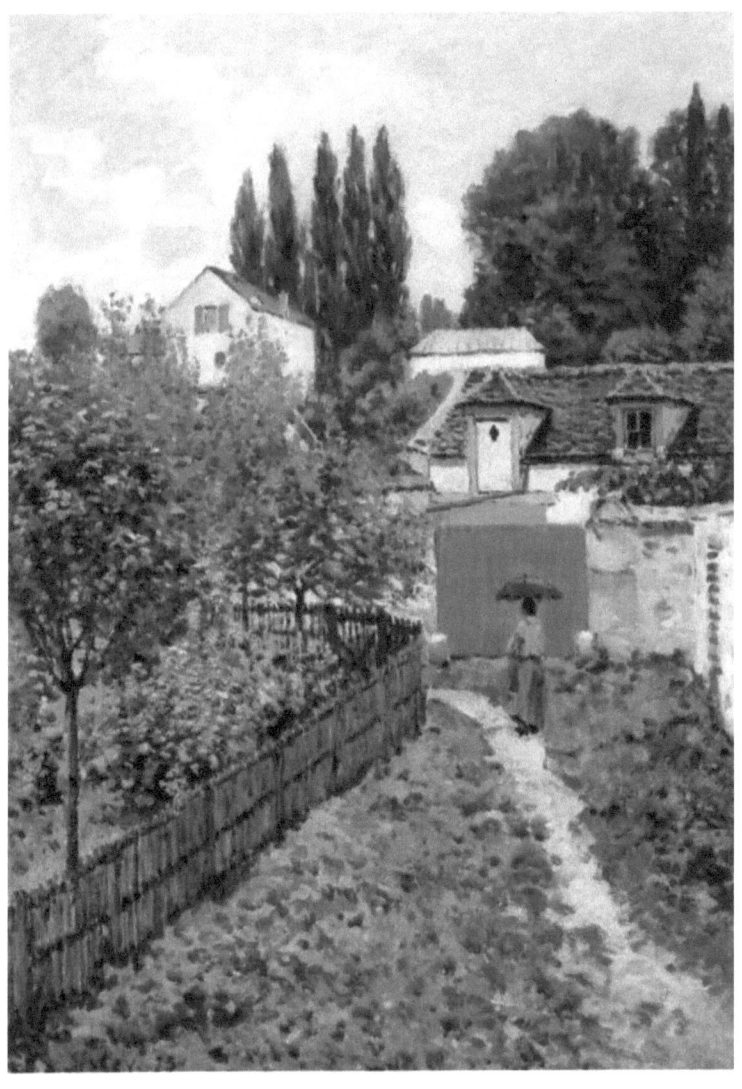

Garden Path in Louveciennes (also known as Chemin
de l'Etarch)
1873, oil on canvas

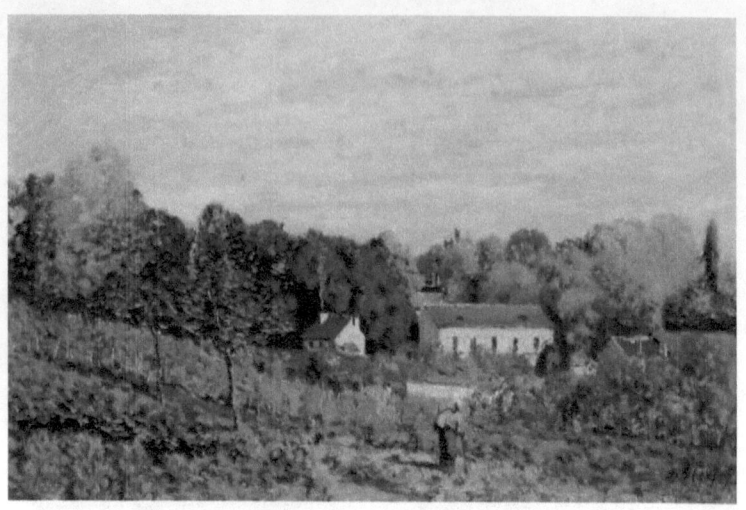

Kitchen Garden at Louveciennes
1873, oil on canvas

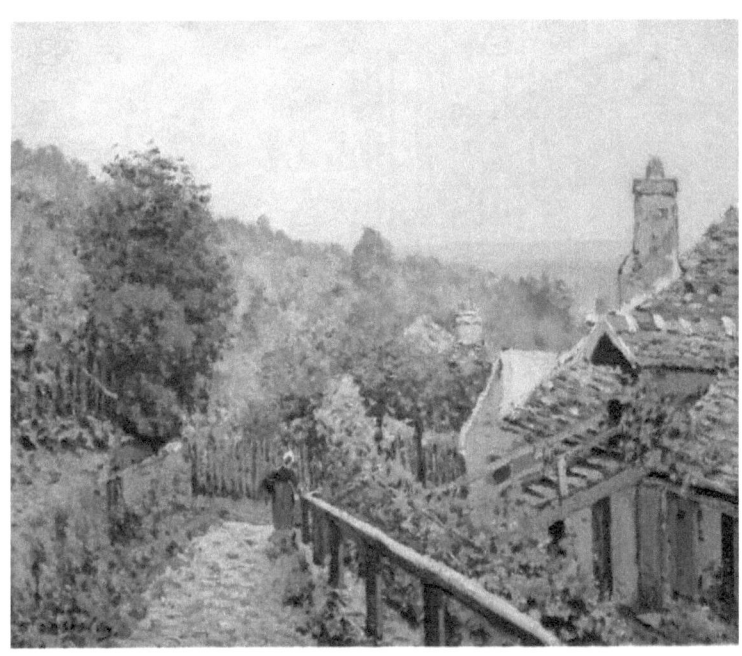

Sentier de la Mi-Cote, Louveciennes
1873, oil on canvas

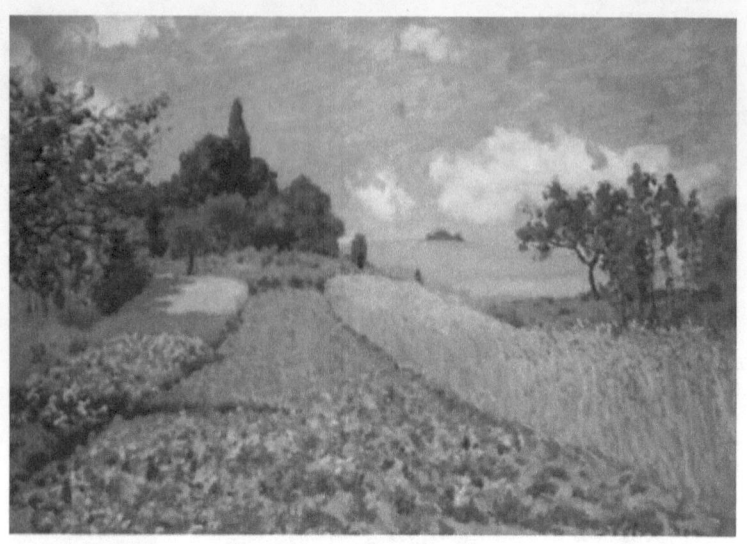

Wheatfields near Argenteuil
1873, oil on canvas

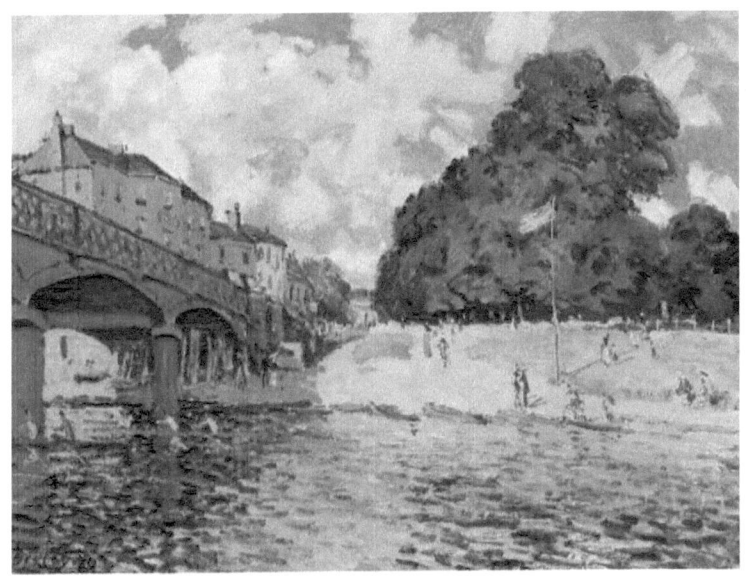

Bridge at Hampton Court
1874, oil on canvas

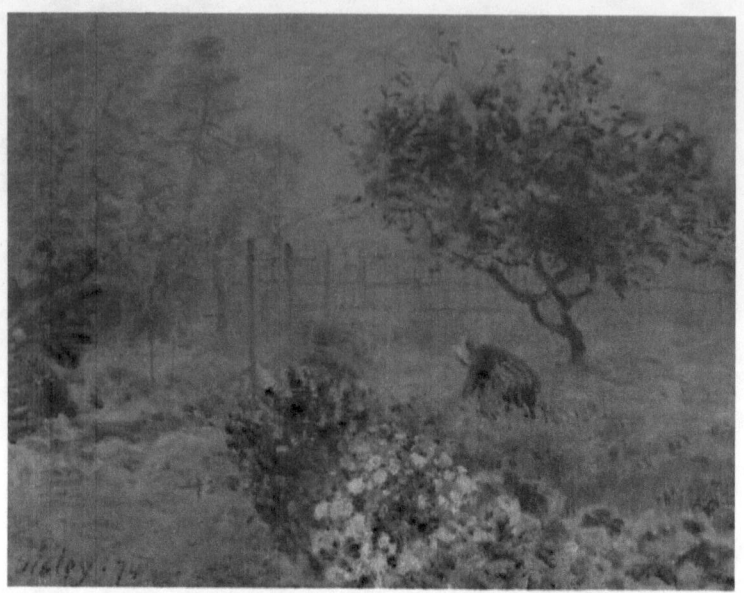

Foggy Morning, Voisins
1874, oil on canvas

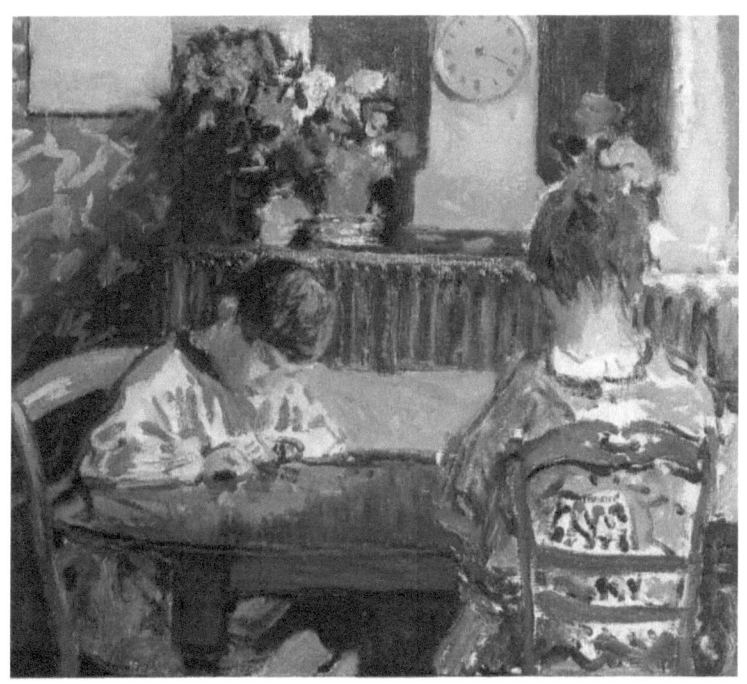

The Lesson
1874, oil on canvas

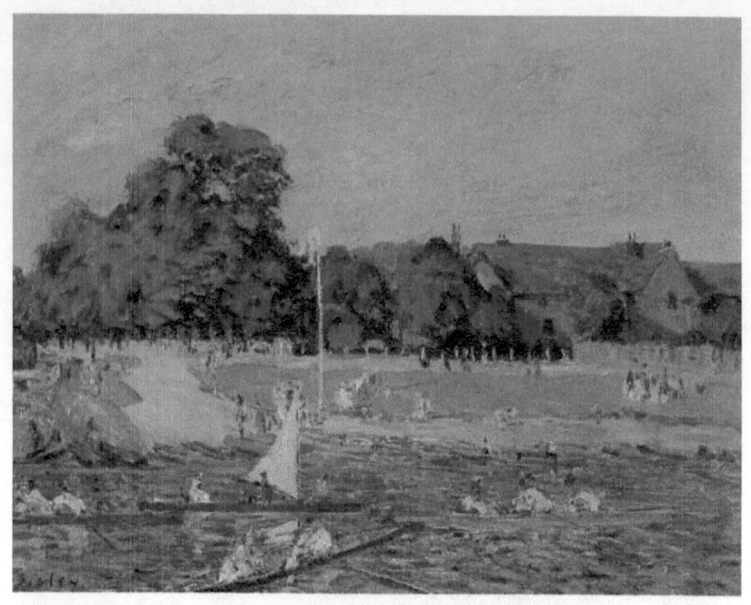

Regatta at Hampton Court
1874, oil on canvas

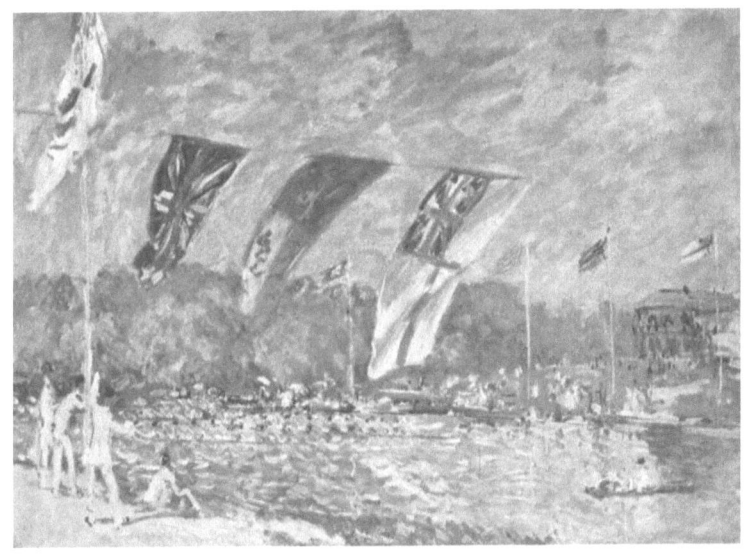

Regatta at Molesey
1874, oil on canvas

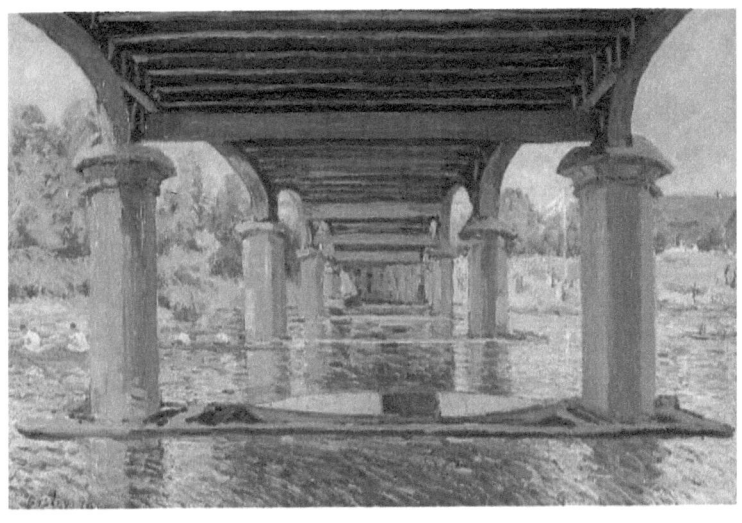

Under the Bridge at Hampton Court
1874, oil on canvas

75

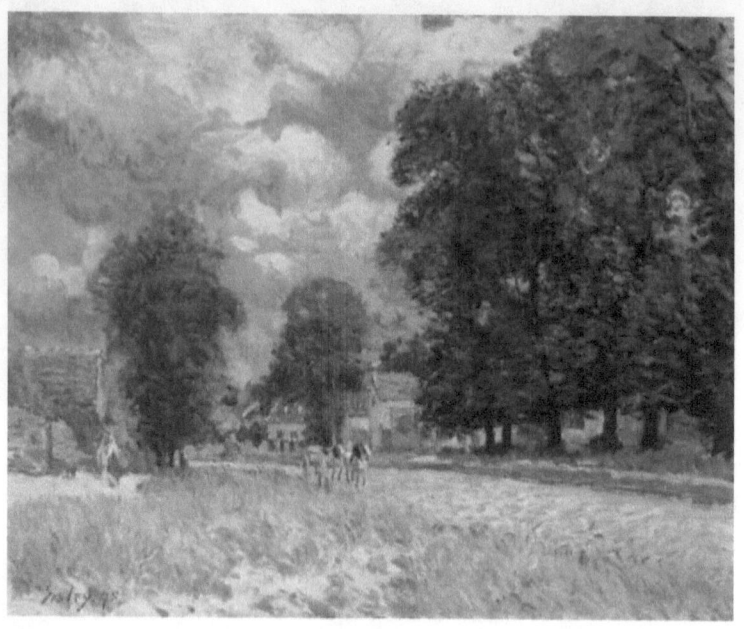

The road to Marly-le-Roi
1875, oil on canvas

The painting dates from the beginning of Sisley's productive time living in Marly-le-Roi, one of the towns in the outskirts of Paris to which some of the Impressionists had moved. In this picture, Sisley has deliberately avoided the beauty spots of the town in which he had now made his home, instead focussing on a scene of everyday life that is filled with its own charm, encapsulating some of the Impressionist ethos.

Before making his home in Marly-le-Roi, Sisley had moved to Louveciennes, having abandoned the Batignolles area of Paris; there he was in close proximity to Renoir in particular, and also to Pissarro and Monet. He had chosen the area in part because of its proximity to Paris, in part because the cost of living there was so much less than in the capital, and in part because he now had a young family to support. However, the clear impetus was the landscape itself: even in Paris, he had favoured scenes involving greenery where possible, and so his move to the less industrialised areas surrounding Paris made perfect sense. The feathered brushstrokes with which he has captured the clouds and the foliage lend the picture a lightness of touch that perfectly demonstrates the reason for which his fellow Impressionists held him in such high regard. Pissarro himself was moved to refer to Sisley as, 'a great and beautiful artist, in my opinion he is a master equal to the greatest'

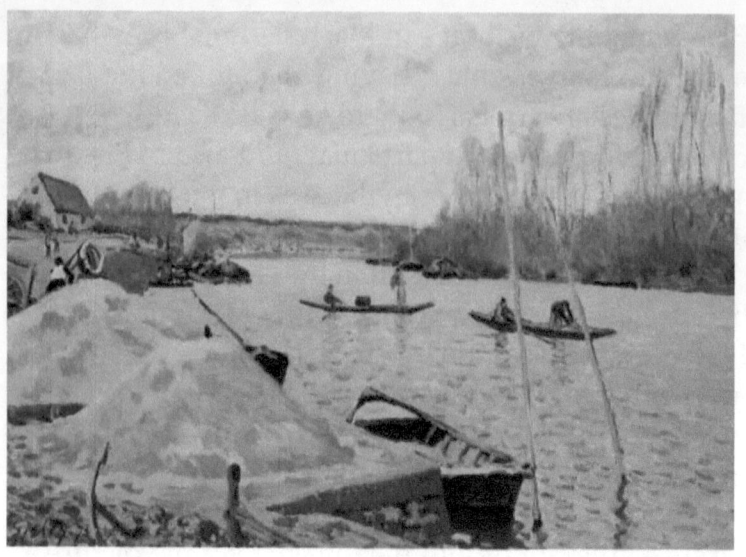

Sand Heaps
1875, oil on canvas

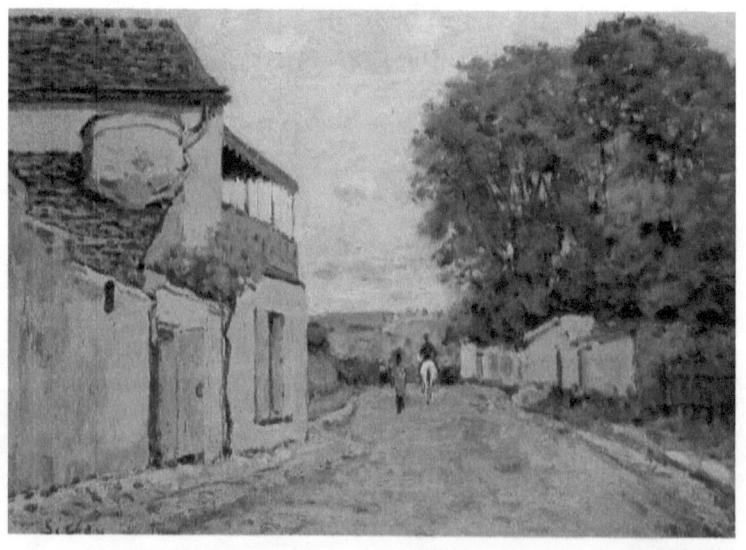

Street in Louveciennes (Rue de la Princesse)
1875, oil on canvas

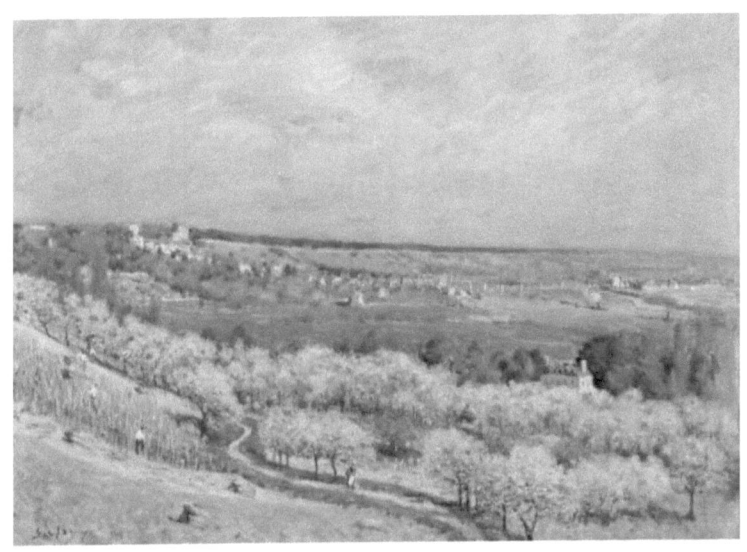

The Terrace at Saint-Germain, Spring
1875, oil on canvas

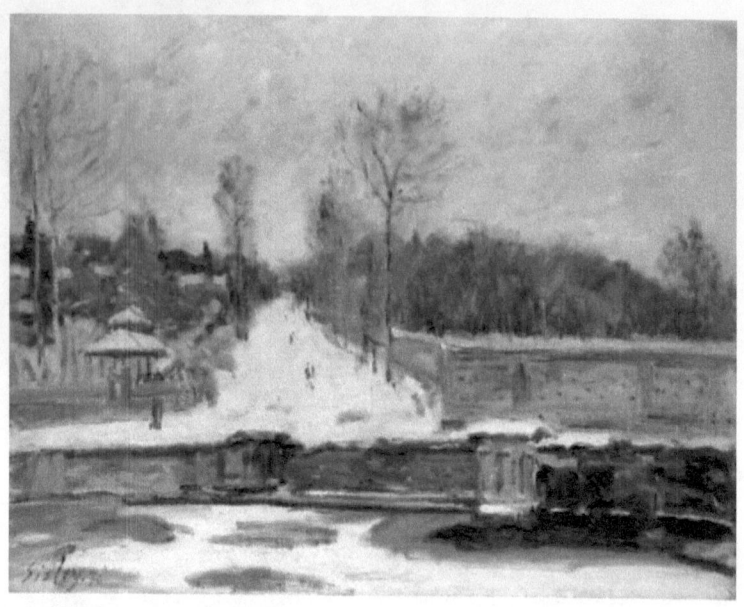

The Watering Place at Marly-le-Roi
1875, Oil on canvas,

The watering place at Marly was constructed during the seventeenth century as part of a large hydraulic system that supplied water to the fountains and pools at the Château de Marly, Louis XIV's country retreat. As part of the king's royal complex, it belonged to the same system as the Marly aqueduct and the Machine the Marly, both of which like the watering place, Sisley painted on several occasions. By the mid-nineteenth century the château and its environs served as mere remnants of courtly life enjoyed more than one hundred years earlier. The buildings and the grounds had been destroyed during the revolution, and by the time of Sisley's arrival, the reservoir of the once-glamorous château functioned as an area in which to wash clothes and a pond from which horses might drink.

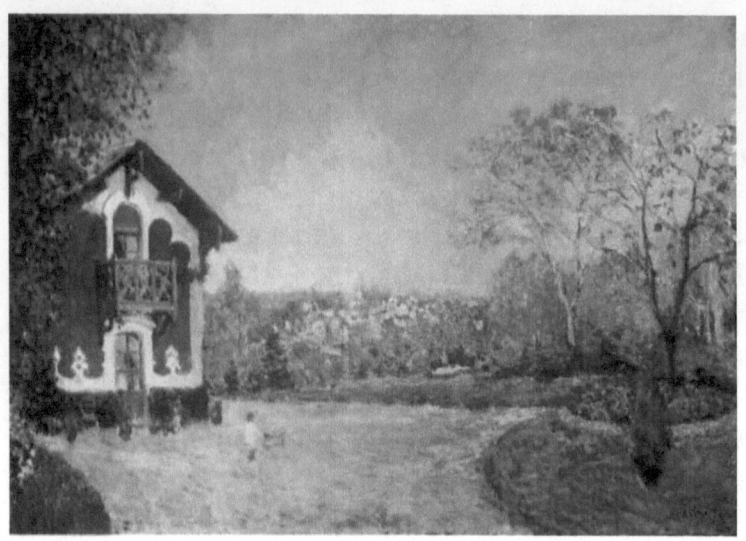

Louveciennes
1876, Oil on canvas,

The pictures Sisley painted are Impressionism of an outstanding order, yet from the connoisseurs' point of view he was never more than a member of the movement who painted like Monet. The fact is that Sisley conveys no sense of an artistic personality. His range of subjects is not great: he painted landscapes only, with an occasional figure. His art in total lacks subjects, techniques or qualities peculiarly his. Yet Sisley's paintings are things of beauty and light, done with ease, the expression of a positive spirit. His unspectacular landscape work alternates between distant and closer views, like the intimate landscapes of the Barbizon school.

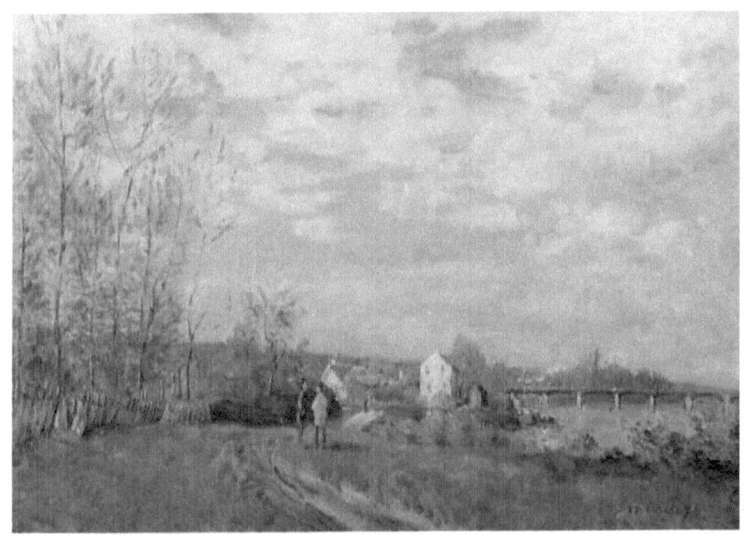

Banks of the Seine at Bougival
1876, oil on canvas

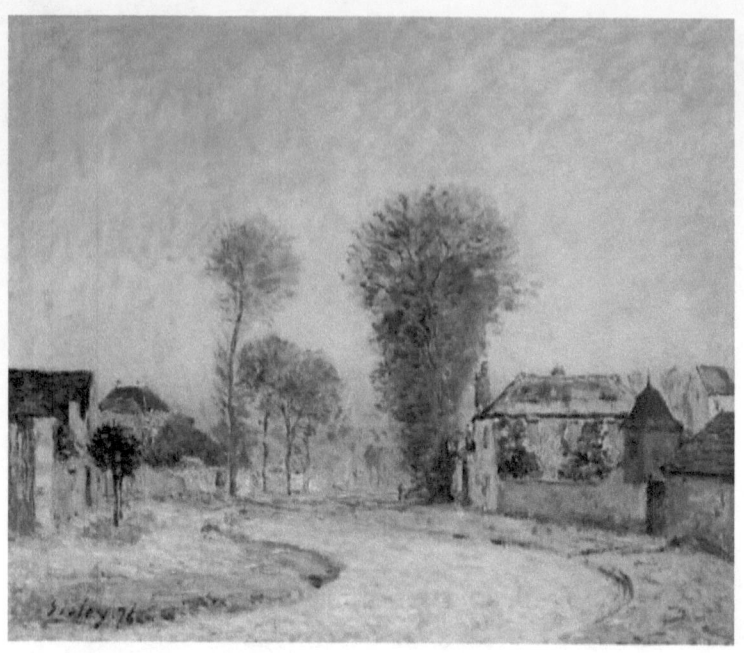

The First Hoarfrost
1876, oil on canvas

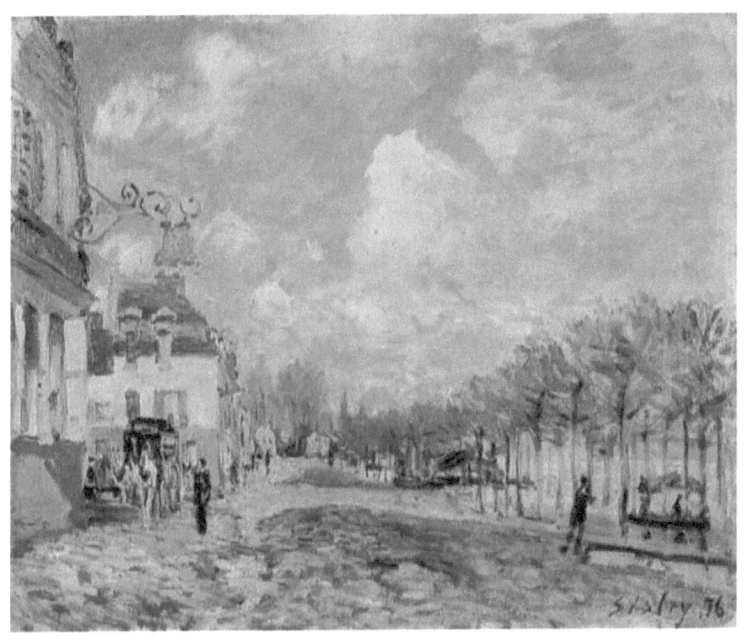

The Flood at Port-Marly
1876, oil on canvas

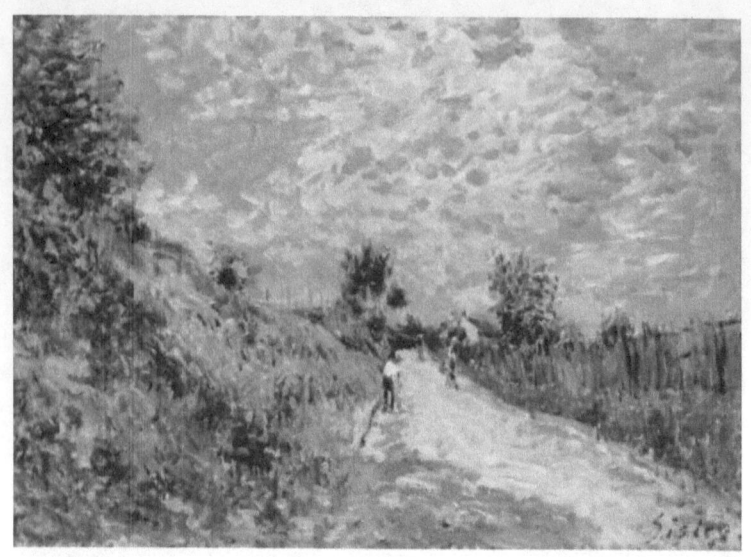

Hill Path
1876, oil on canvas

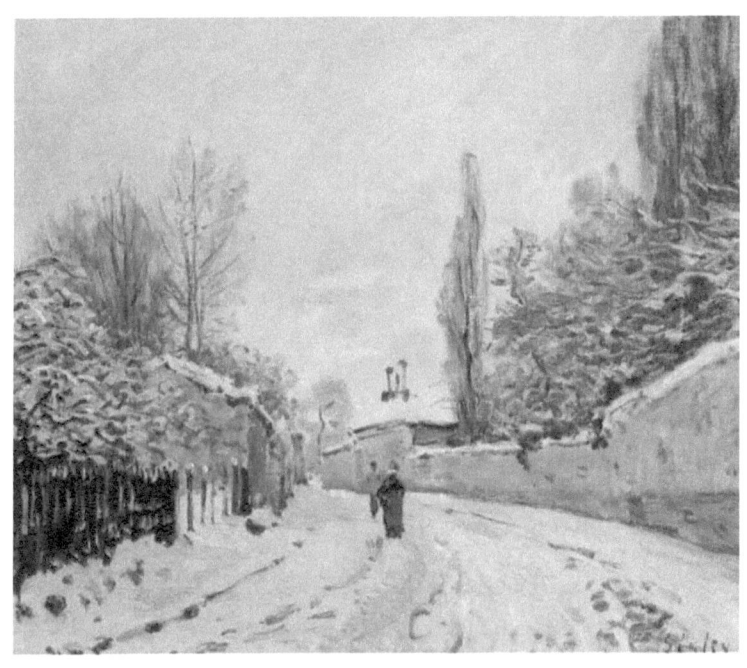

Road under Snow, Louveciennes
1876, oil on canvas

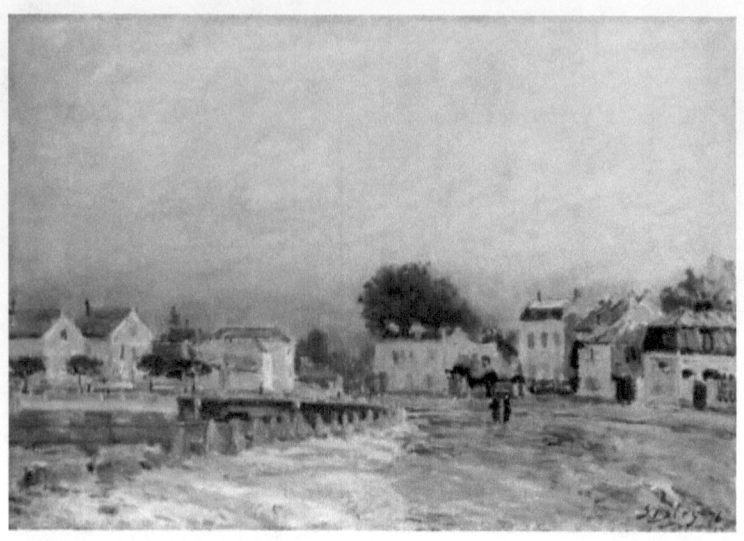

The Watering Place at Mary-le-Roi with Hoarfrost
1876, Oil on canvas, 38 x 55 cm

Sisley lived in Marly-le-Roi, west of Paris, from 1875-77.
There he painted numerous pictures of the elegant
watering-place, one of the few remains of Louis XIV's
summer palace, which was destroyed in 1793.

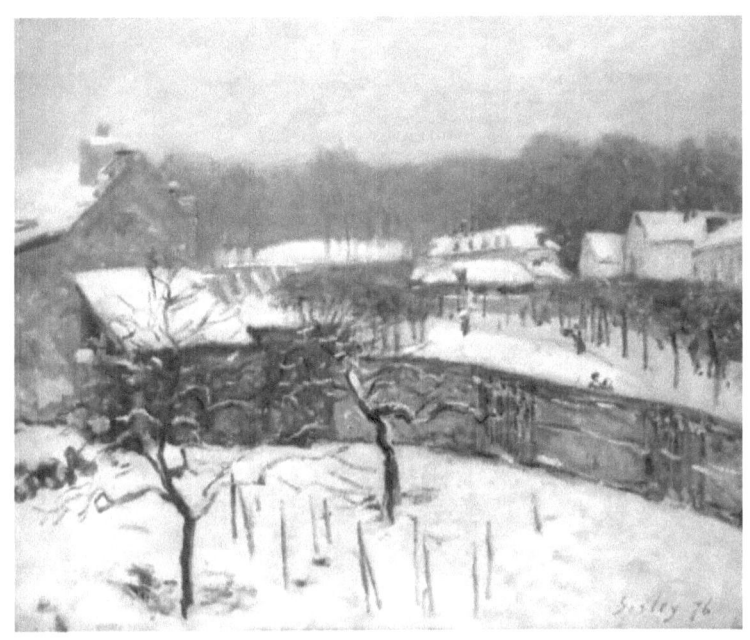

Snow Effect at Louveciennes
1876, Oil on canvas

Sisley painted the waters of the Seine at Bougival or
Marly as sensitively as the nuances of snow colour in
Pissarro's beloved lanes and gardens of Louveciennes.

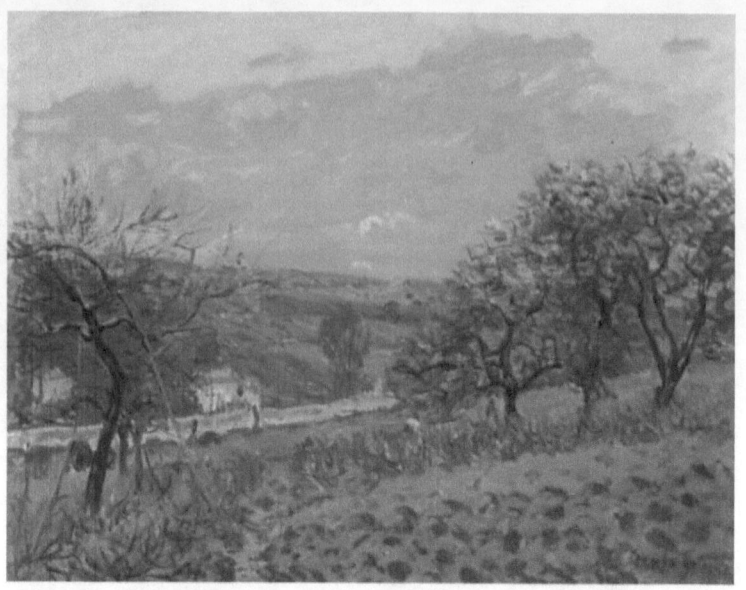

Bougival
1876, Oil on canvas

The present landscape painting depicts the countryside at Bougival, a picturesque suburban enclave in the lush valley of the Seine, less than twenty kilometers west of Paris. The canvas was painted in 1876, when Sisley was living in nearby Marly-le-Roi. Both Sisley and Monet had settled in Bougival in the late 1860s; Renoir had visited the town frequently during the summer of 1869, painting alongside Monet at the popular bathing establishment, La Grenouillère. When the Franco-Prussian War broke out in the autumn of 1870, Sisley took refuge in Paris, and Monet fled Bougival for England. Sisley's house at Bougival was pillaged by the Prussian army, and the contents of his studio were largely destroyed. When Sisley and his family returned to the Seine valley late in 1871, they joined Pissarro at Louveciennes rather than returning to Bougival; in the first weeks of 1875, they moved to Marly-le-Roi, where they remained for the next two and a half years. Sisley's stay in Marly was the period of some of his greatest landscapes

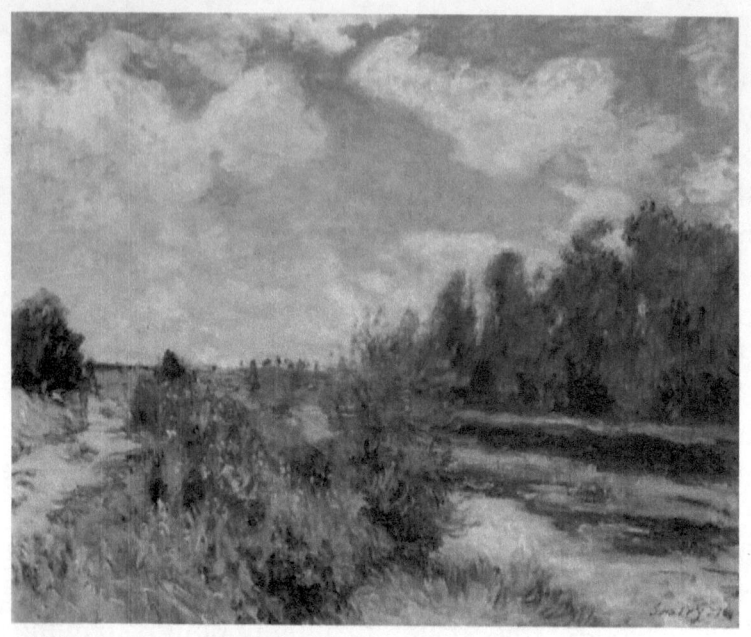

The Seine at Bougival
1876, oil on canvas

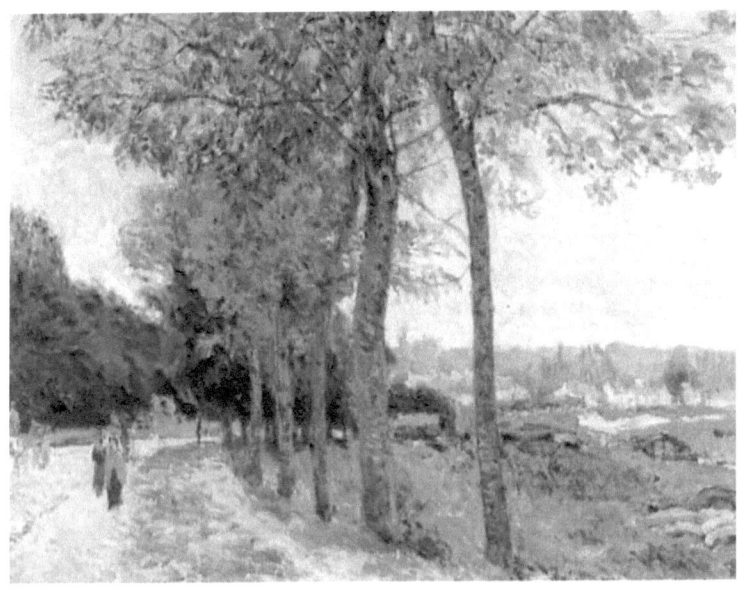

The Seine at Marly
1876, oil on canvas

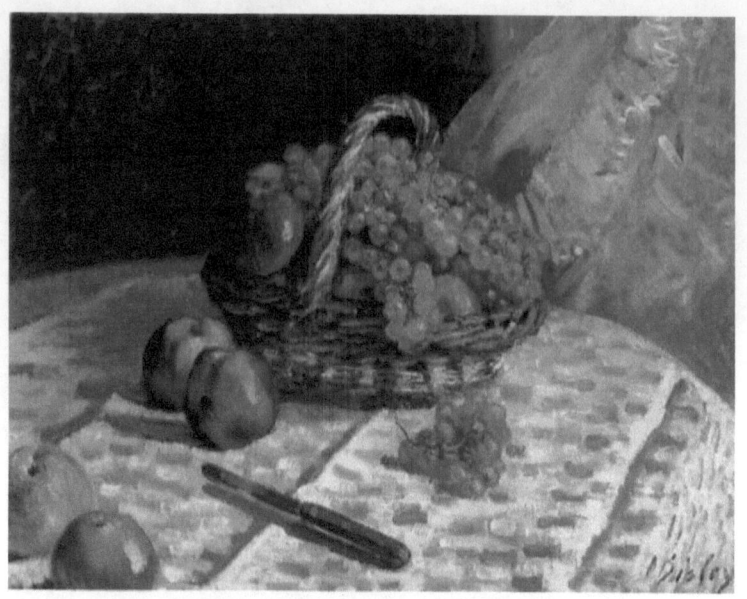

Still Life - Apples and Grapes
1876, oil on canvas

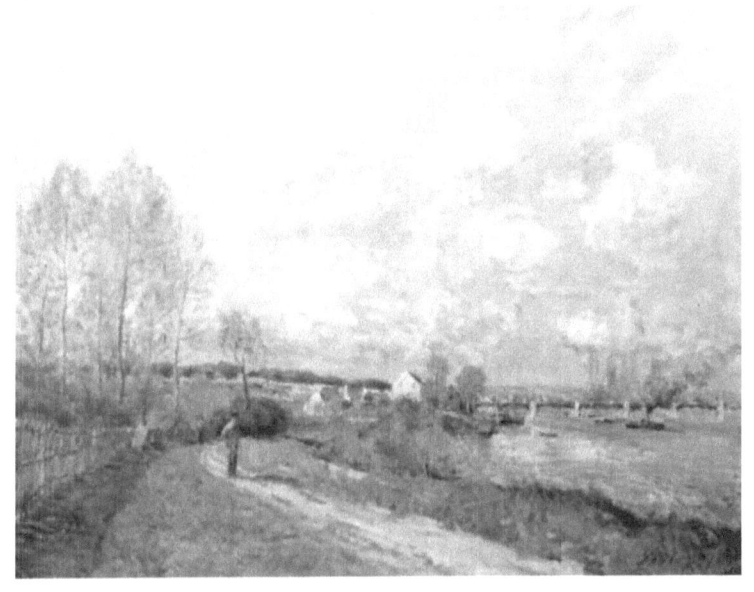

Summer at Bougival
1876, oil on canvas

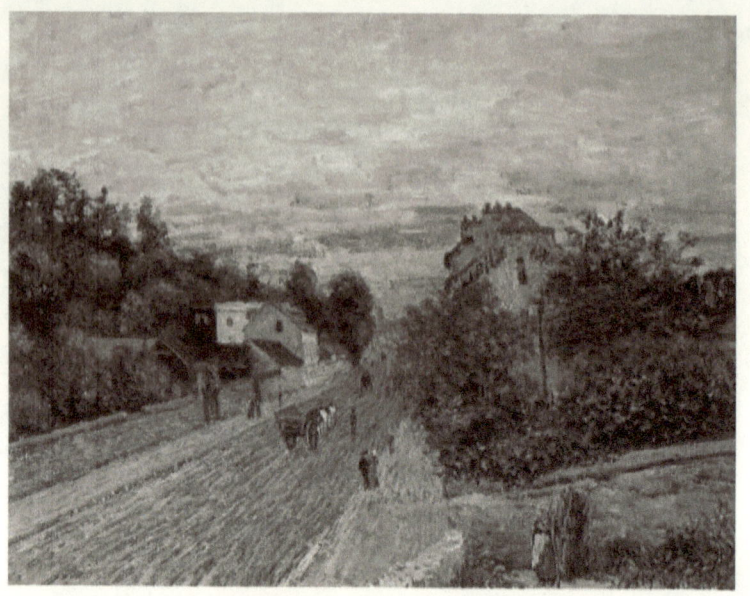

Sunset at Port-Marly
1876, oil on canvas

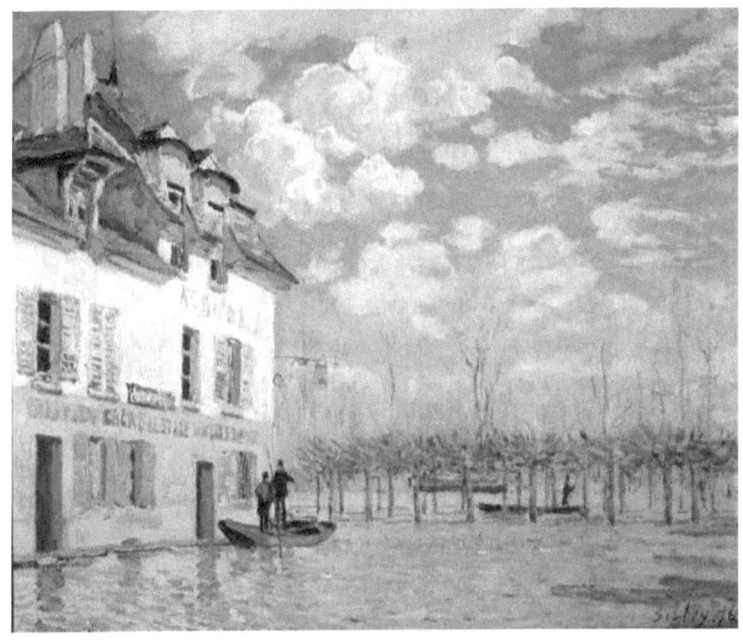

Flood at Port-Marly
1876, Oil on canvas

Working from a boat during a catastrophic flood in the
spring of 1876, Sisley painted the corner of a wine
merchant's house in the small town of Port-Marly on
the banks of the Seine. Sisley's portrayal of the sky is
comparable with those of the great Dutch landscape
painters of the 17th century (Jan van Goyen, Salomon
van Ruysdael, and Jacob van Ruisdael). Equally
influential were the works of the English painters
Constable and Turner, with which he had become
familiar in London.

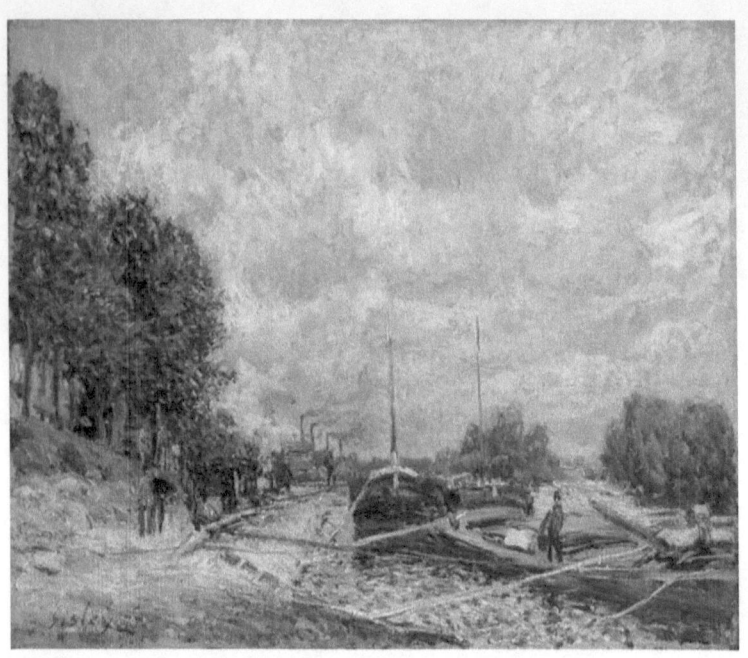

Barges at Billancourt
1877, oil on canvas

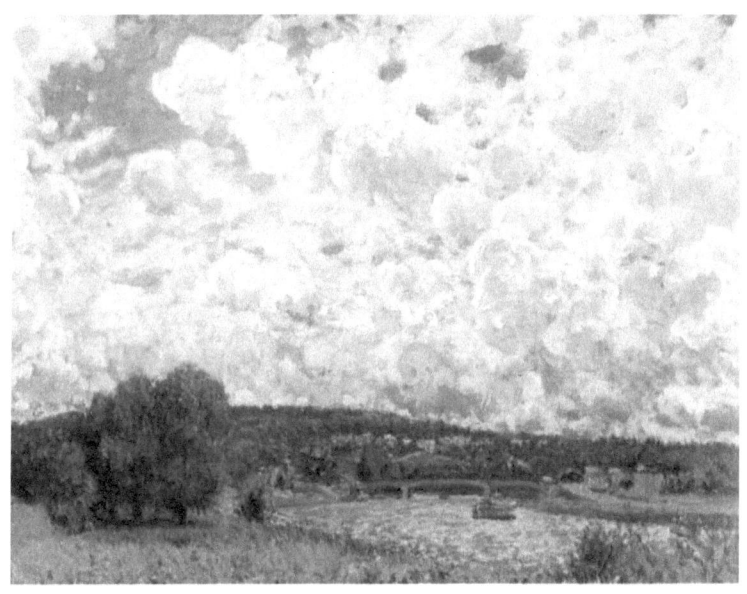

The Seine at Suresnes
1877, oil on canvas

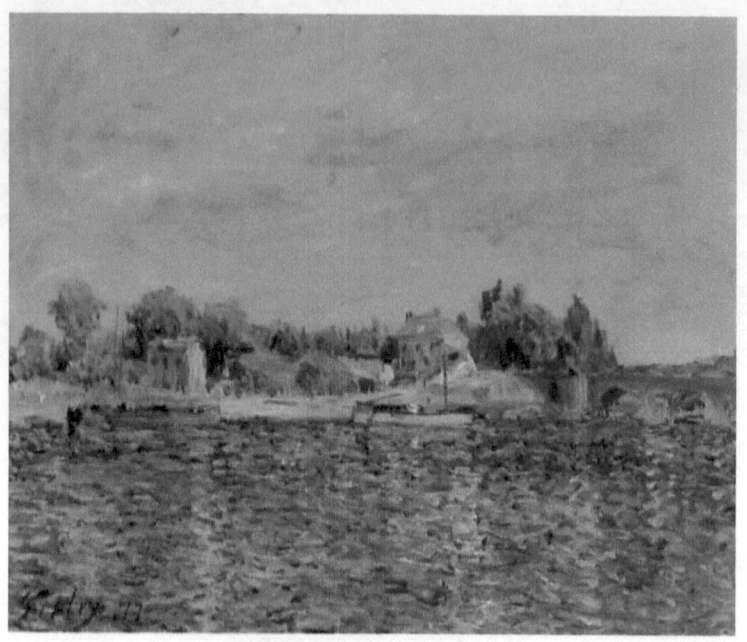

Sevres Bridge
1877, oil on canvas

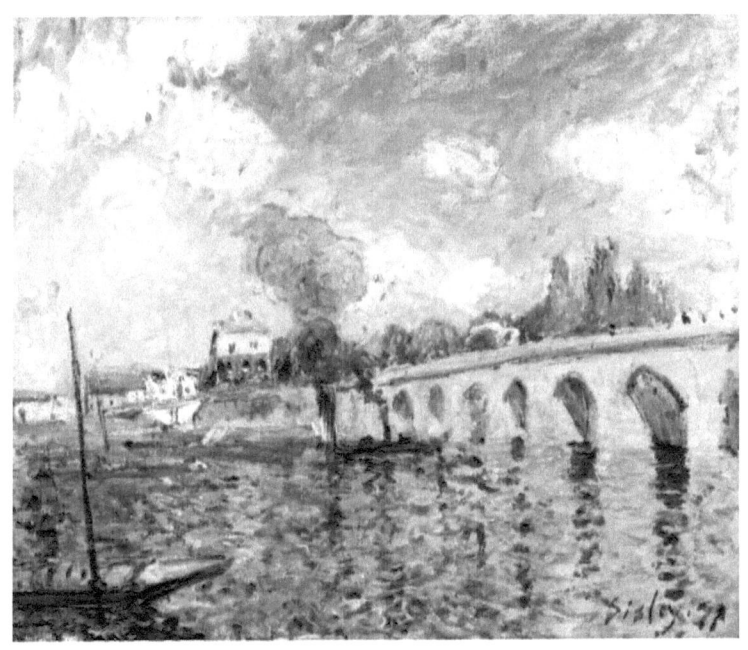

The Sevres Bridge
1877, oil on canvas

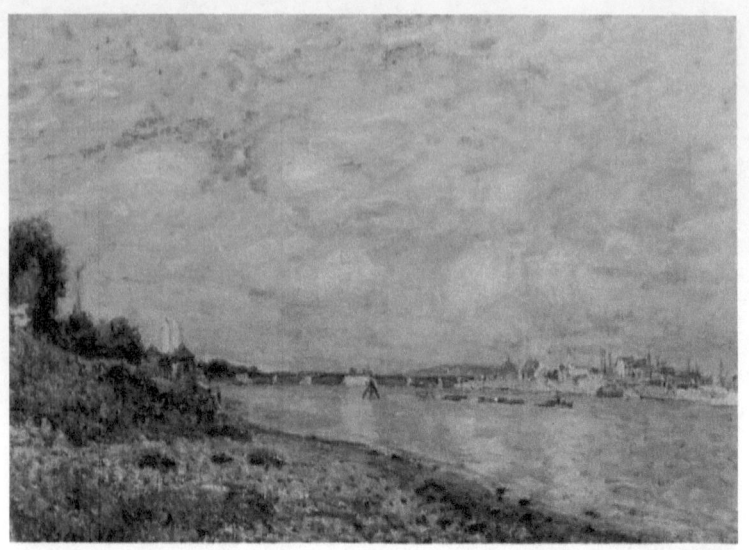

Bougival
1878, oil on canvas

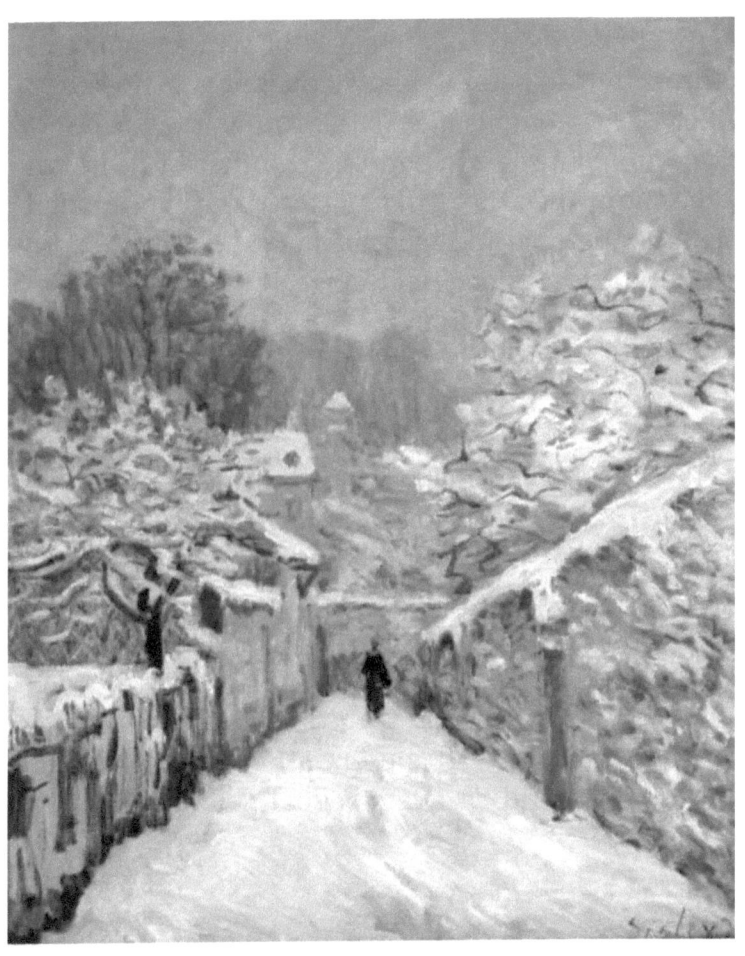

Snow at Louveciennes
1878, Oil on canvas,

Many of Sisley's works appear to be typical examples of Impressionism, and this snow-covered landscape, which dates from his most successful period, is no exception. In his treatment of the mother-of-pearl tones of the snow, the artist truly mastered the evocation of the imponderable and the transitory. The painting is one of the most poetic renderings of the fragile and ephemeral world of snow.

Sisley was a British-French landscape painter. Born in Paris to English parents, he began painting as an amateur. His early style was much influenced by Camille Corot. He became associated with Claude Monet and Pierre-Auguste Renoir and with them became one of the founders of Impressionism. His works, mostly landscapes, are distinguished from those of his colleagues by their softly harmonious values. His family was ruined by the Franco-Prussian War, and his life was a constant struggle against poverty. Not until after his death did his talent begin to be widely recognized.

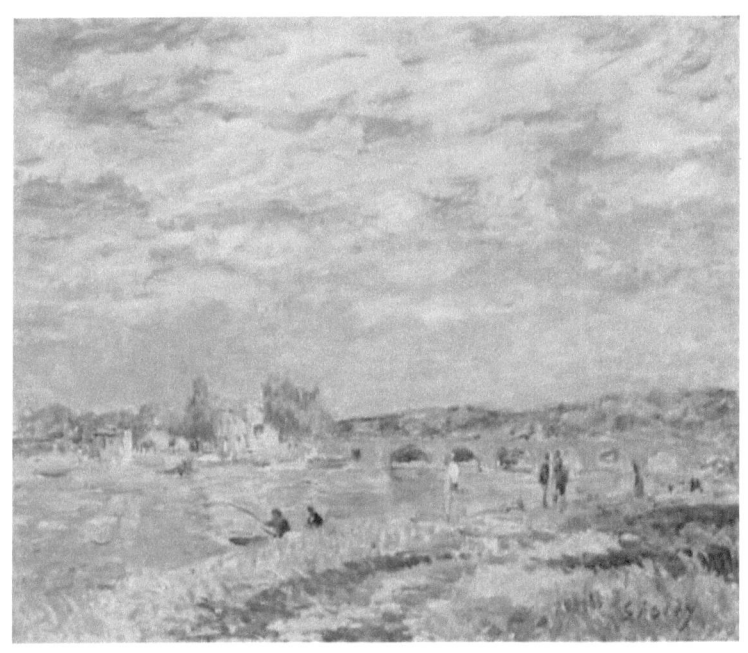

Bridge at Sevres
1879, oil on canvas

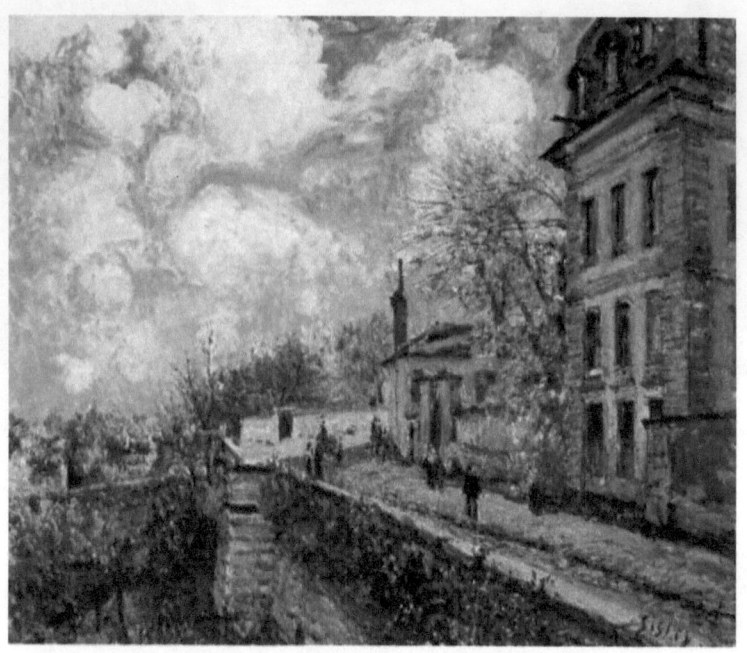

The Factory at Sevres
1879, oil on canvas

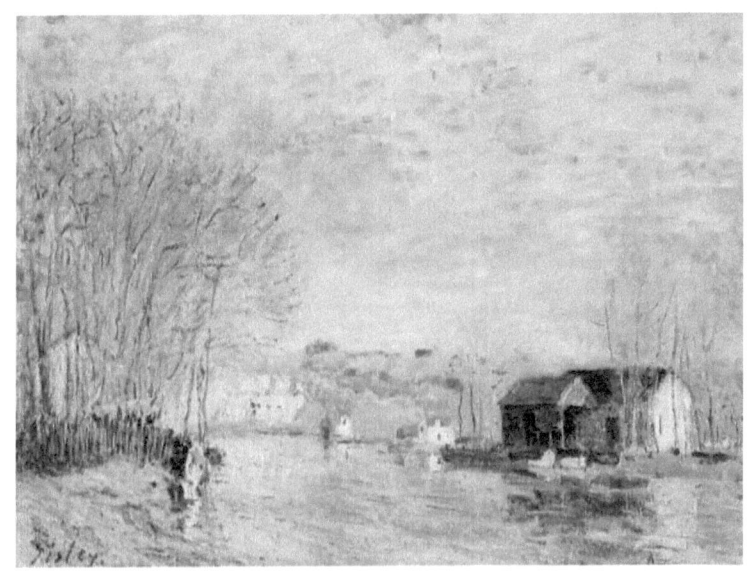

High Waters at Moret-sur-Loing
1879, oil on canvas

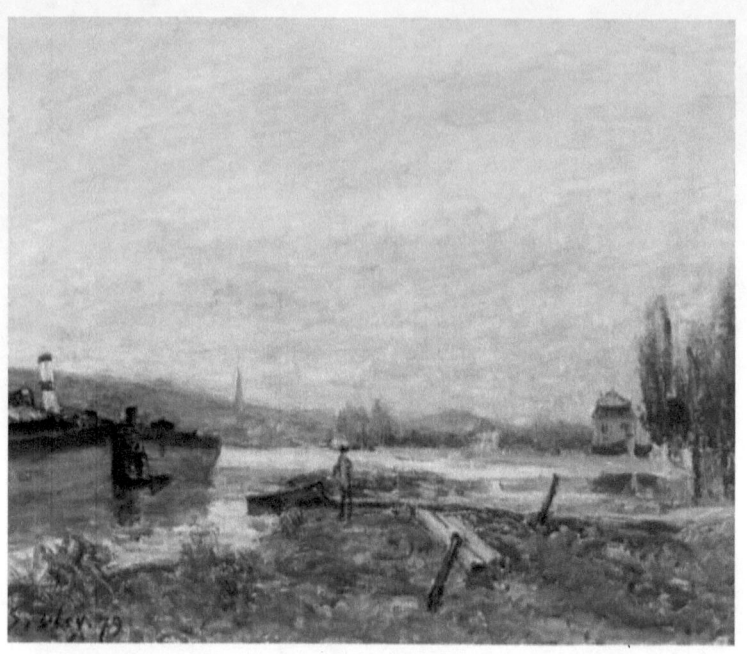

Saint-Cloud, Banks of the Seine
1879, oil on canvas

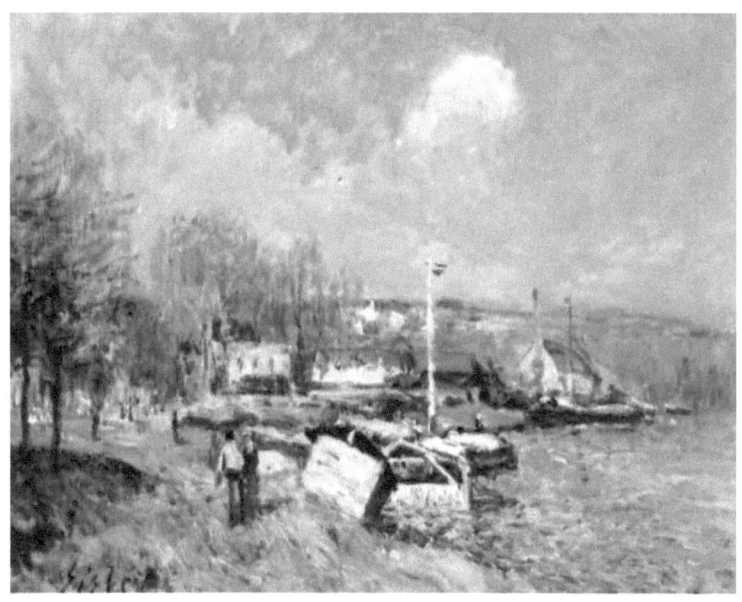

The Seine at Port-Marly
1879, oil on canvas

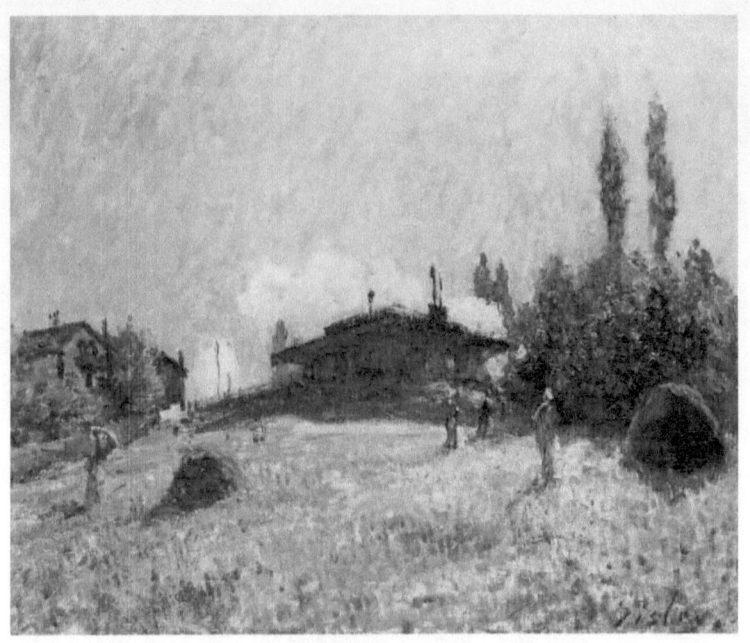

Station at Sevres
1879, oil on canvas

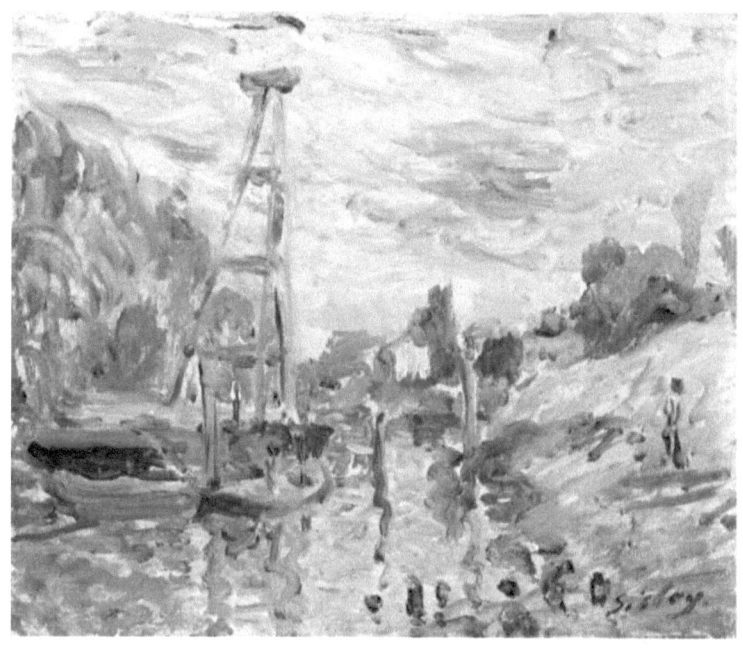

Bateau de Charge sur le Loing
1880, oil on canvas

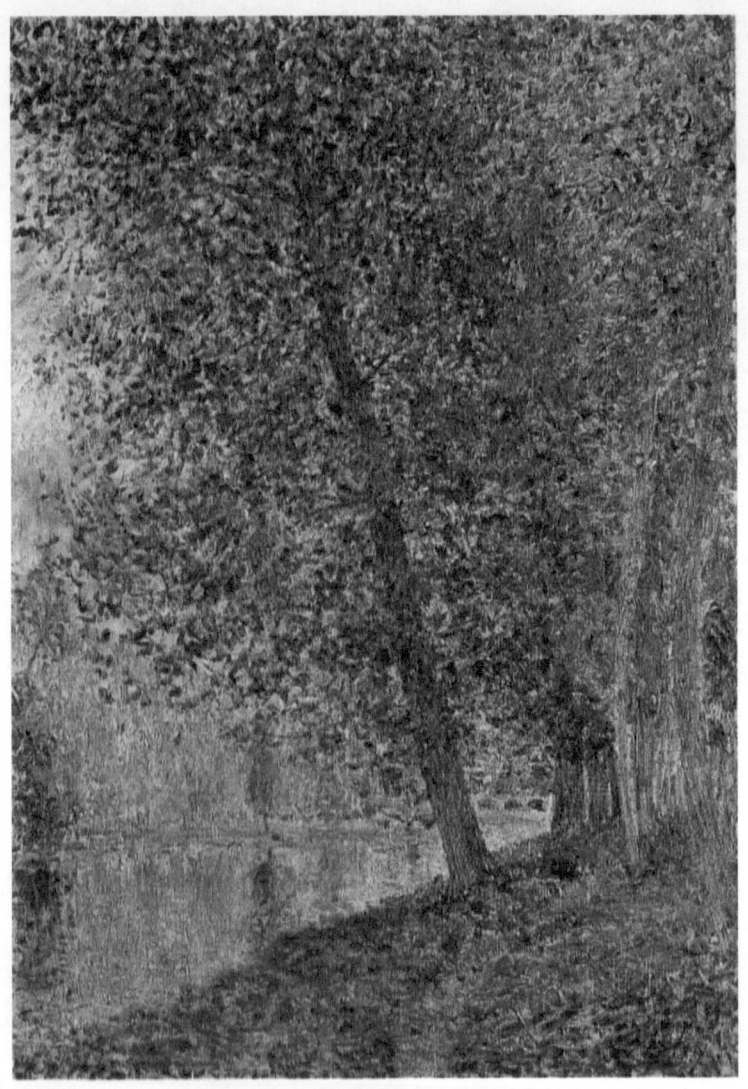

Banks of the Loing, Autumn
1880, oil on canvas

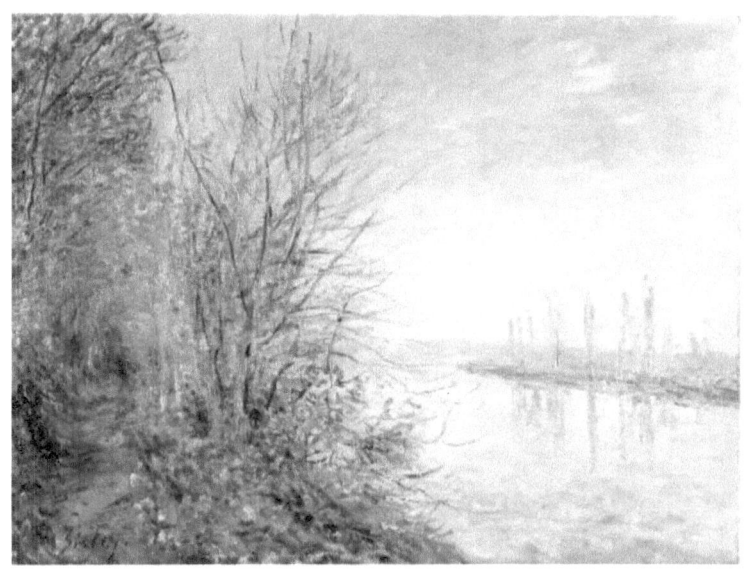

The Chemin de By through Woods at Rouches-
Courtaut, St. Martin's, Summer
1880, oil on canvas

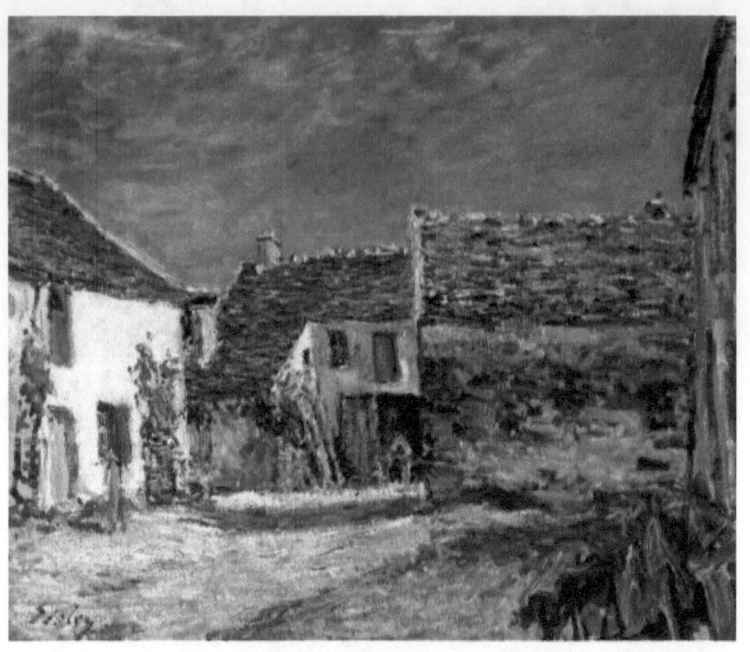

Farmyard near Moret - July Sun
1880, oil on canvas

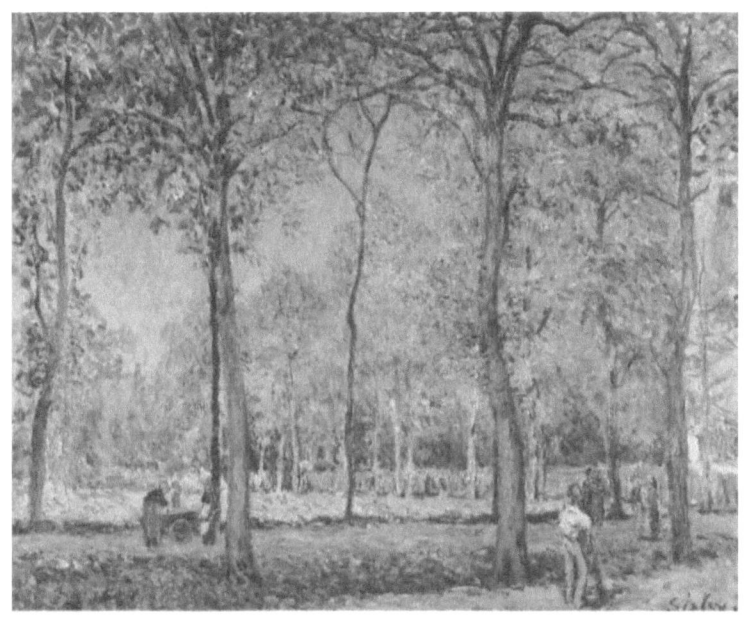

The Forest at Boulogne
1880, oil on canvas

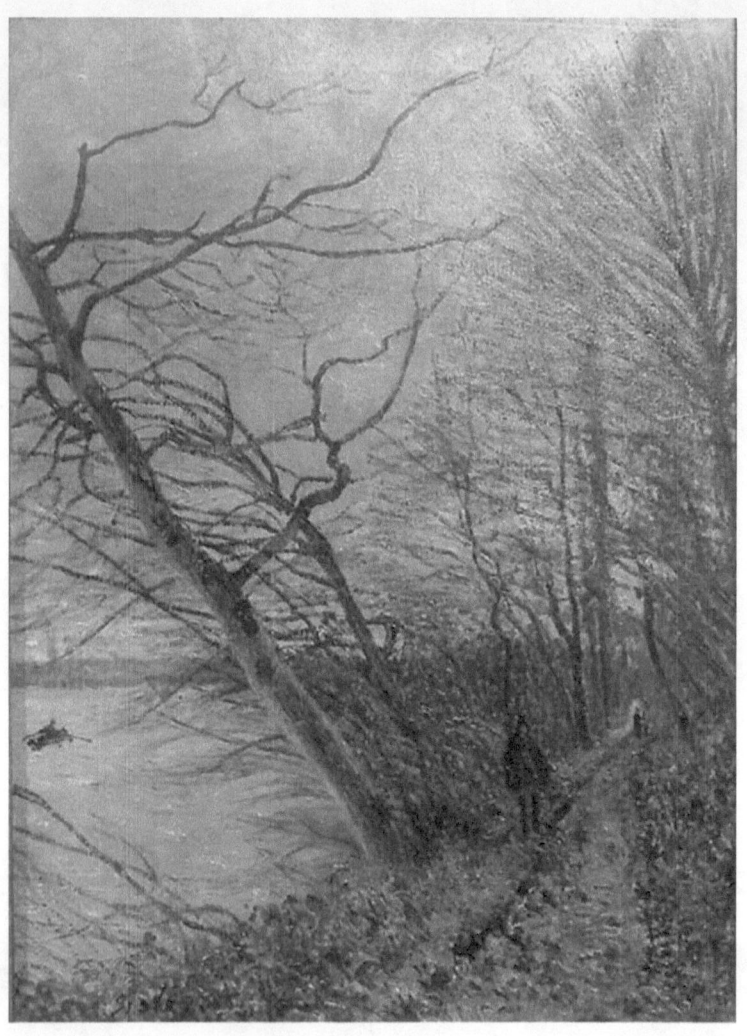

Le Bois des Roches - Veneux- Nadon
1880, oil on canvas

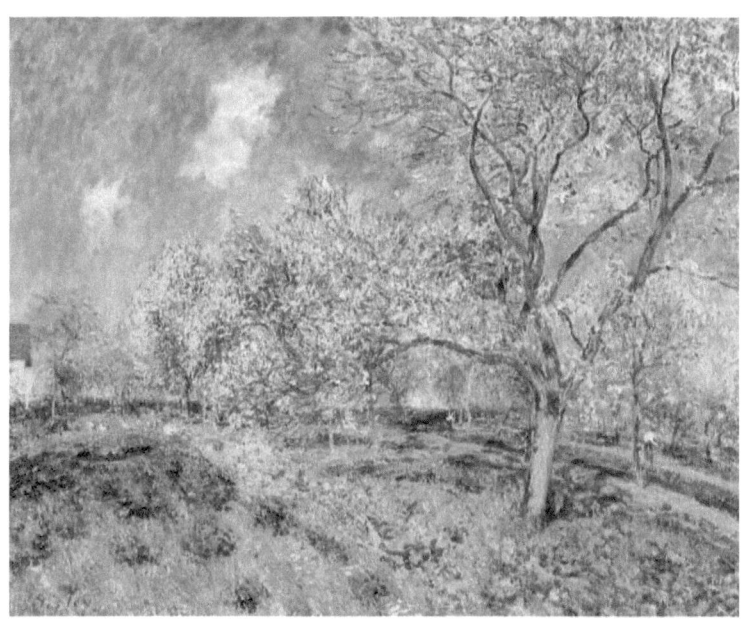

Spring at Veneux
1880, oil on canvas

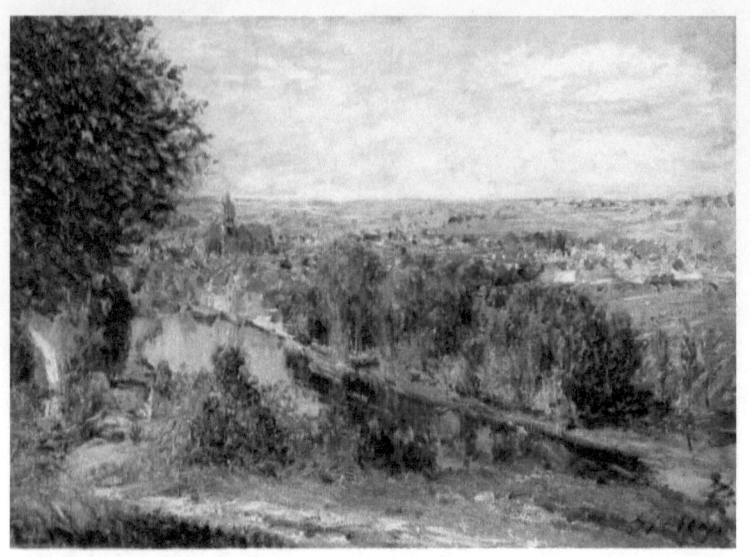

View of Moret
1880, oil on canvas

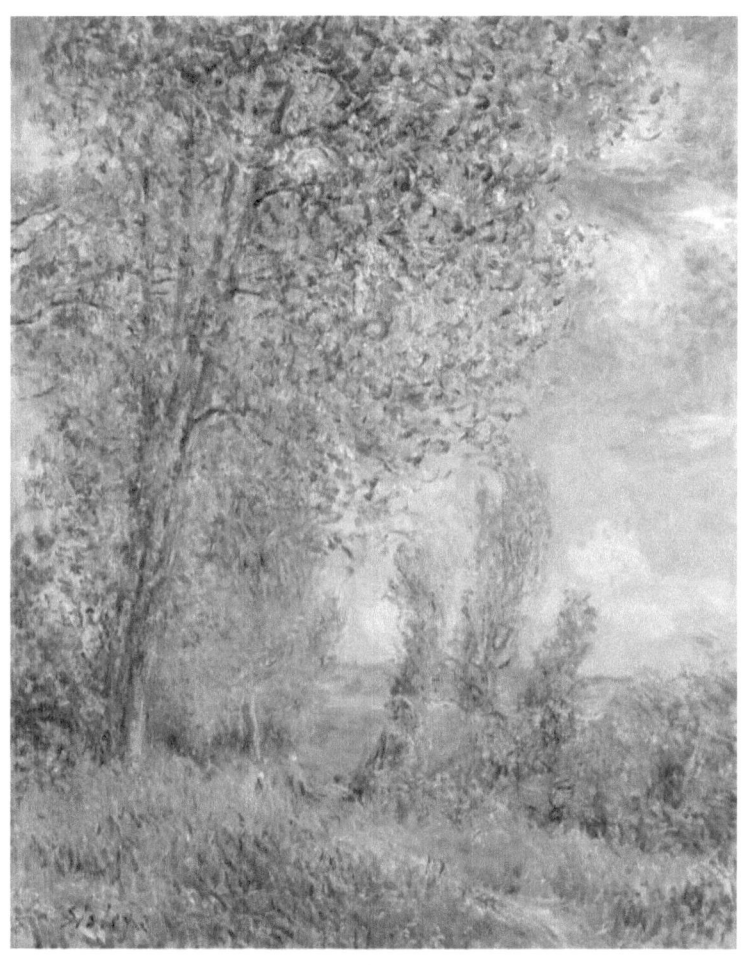

Windy Afternoon in May
1880, oil on canvas

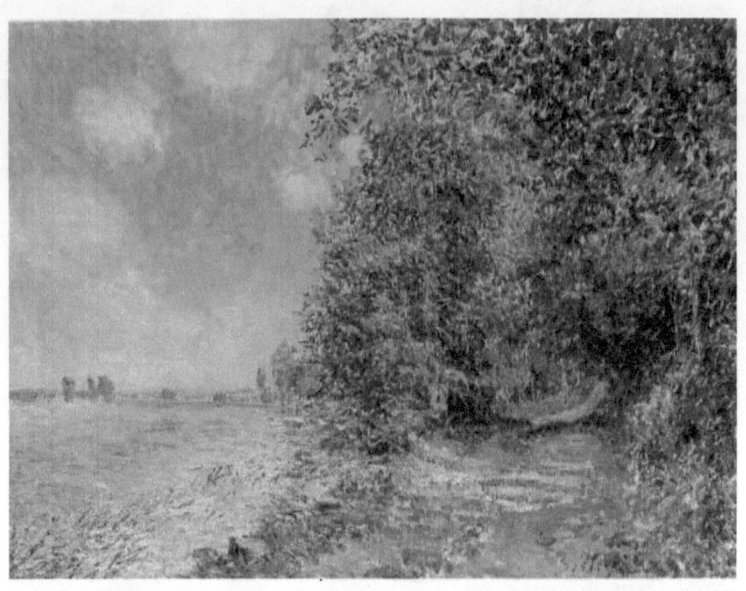

An August Afternoon near Veneux
1881, oil on canvas

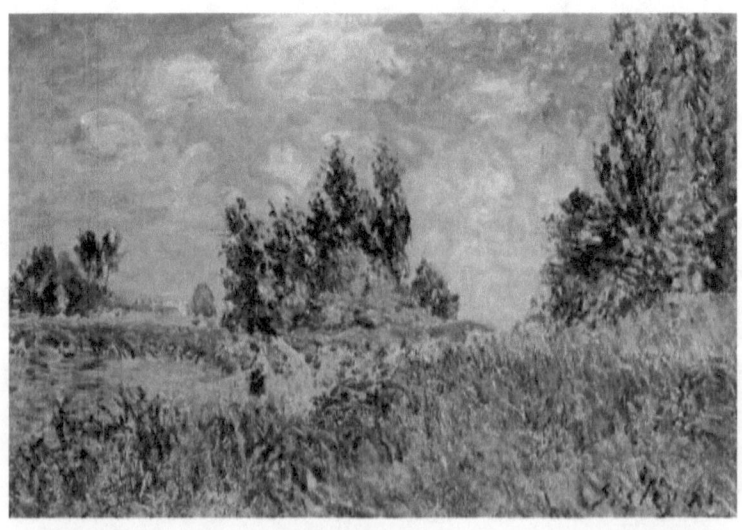

Landscape - The Banks of the Loing at Saint-Mammes
1881, oil on canvas

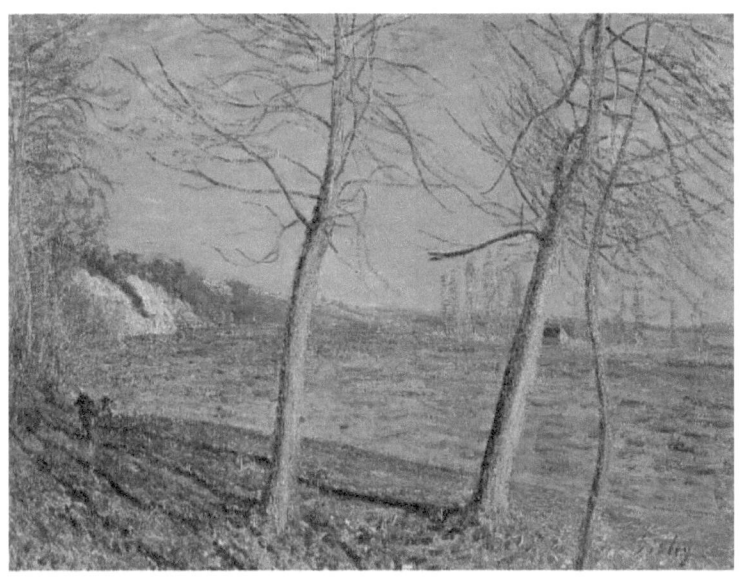

Riverbank at Veneux
1881, oil on canvas

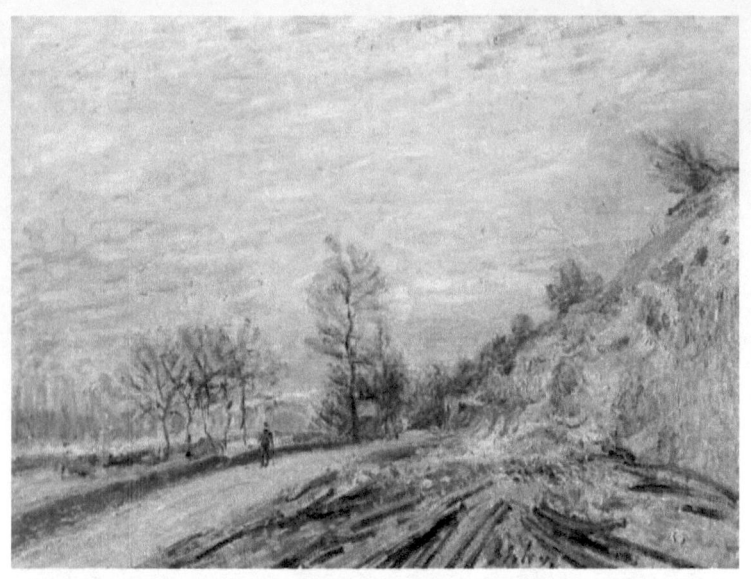

On the Road from Moret
1882, oil on canvas

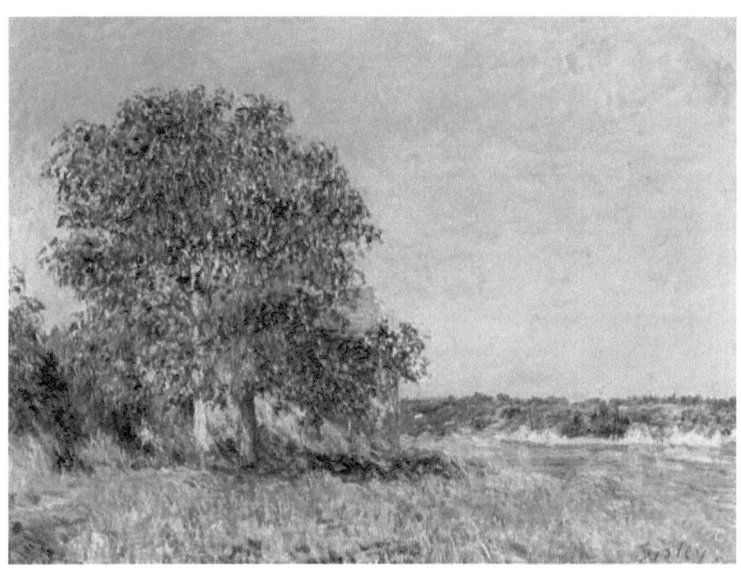

The Plain of Thomery and the Village of Champagne
1882, oil on canvas

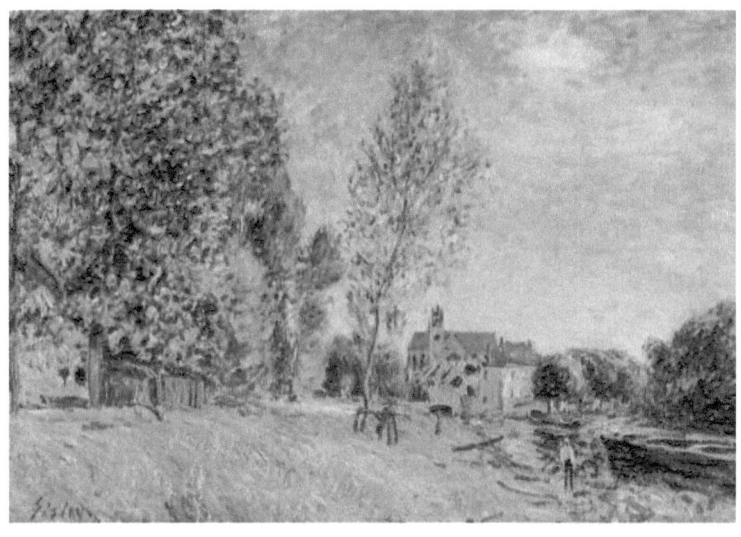

Matratat's Boatyard, Moret-sur-Loing
1883, oil on canvas

123

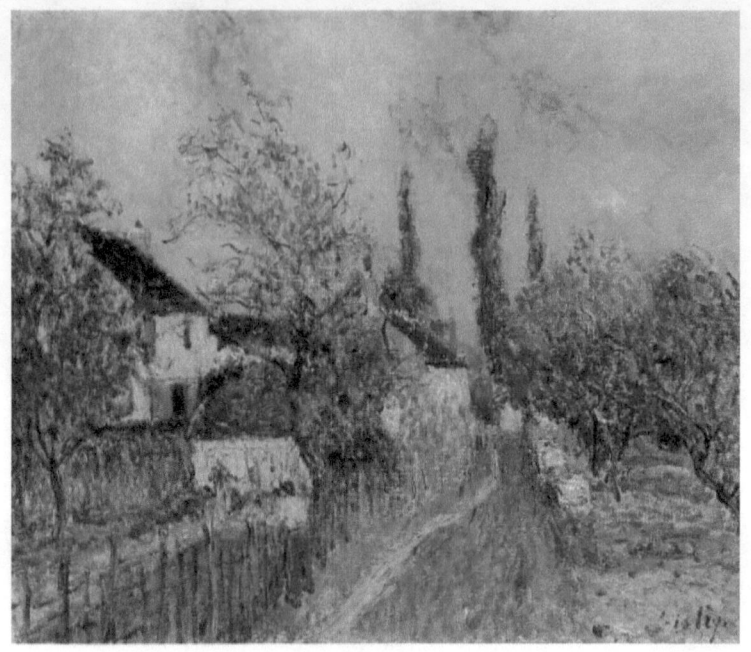

Path at Sablons
1883, oil on canvas

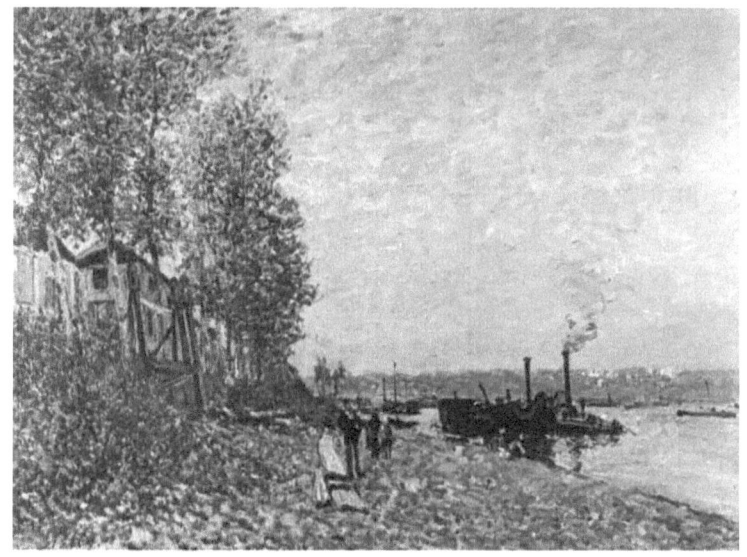

The Tugboat
1883, oil on canvas

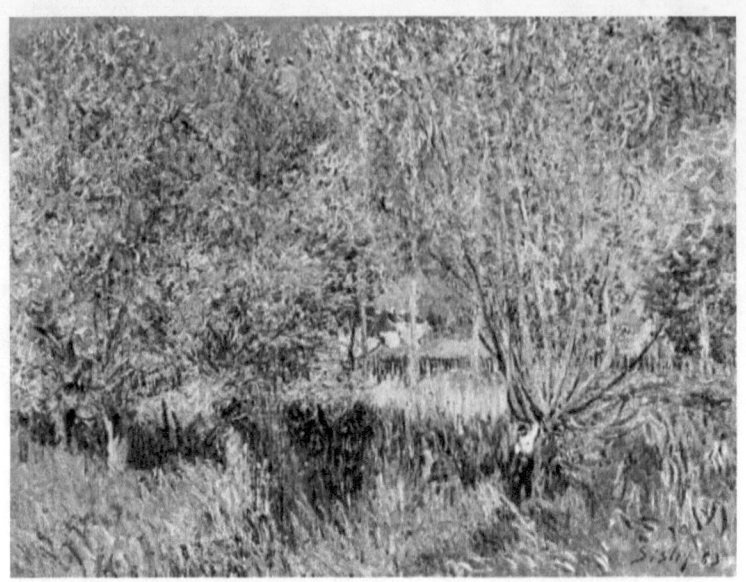

Willows on the Banks of the Orvanne
1883, oil on canvas

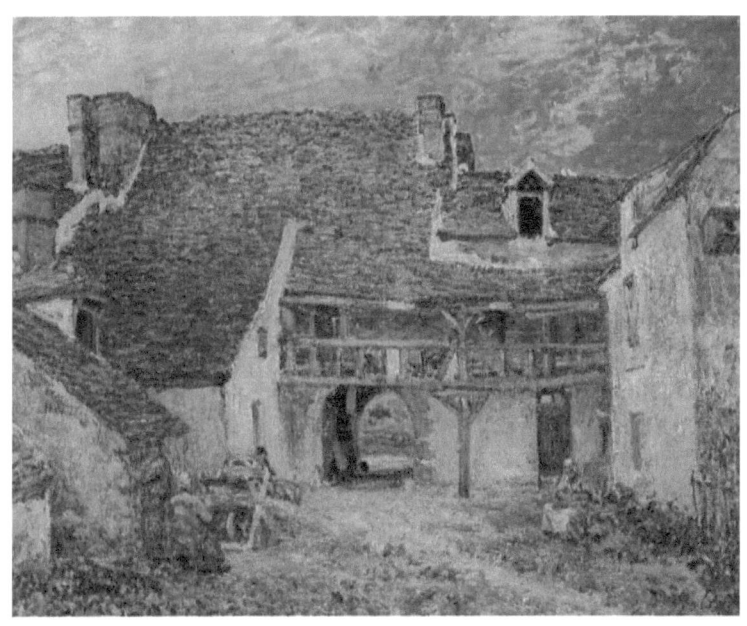

Courtyard of a Farm at Saint-Mammes
1884, oil on canvas

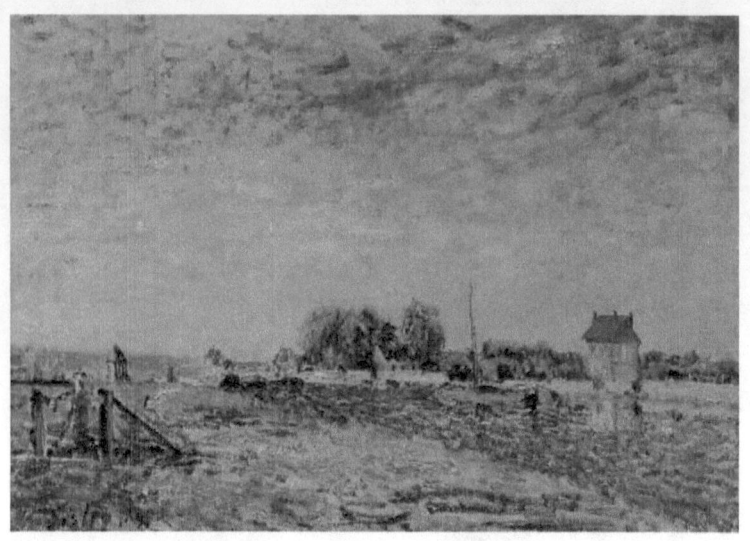

The Loing Canal
1884, oil on canvas

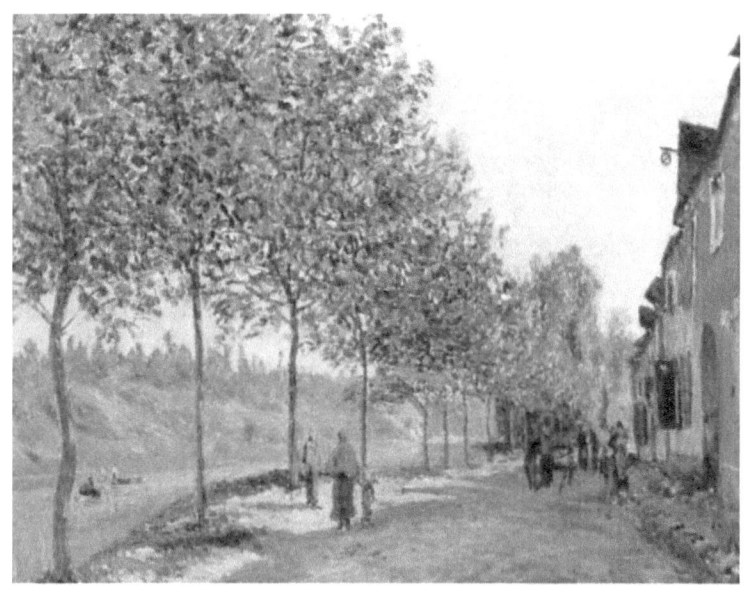

Morning in June (also known as Saint-Mammes et les
Coteaux de la Celle)
1884, oil on canvas

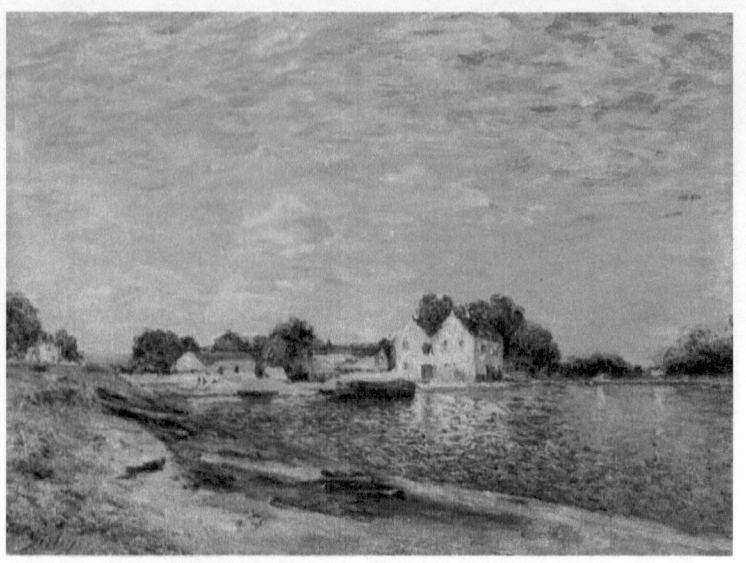

Saint-Mammes, on the Banks of the Loing
1884, oil on canvas

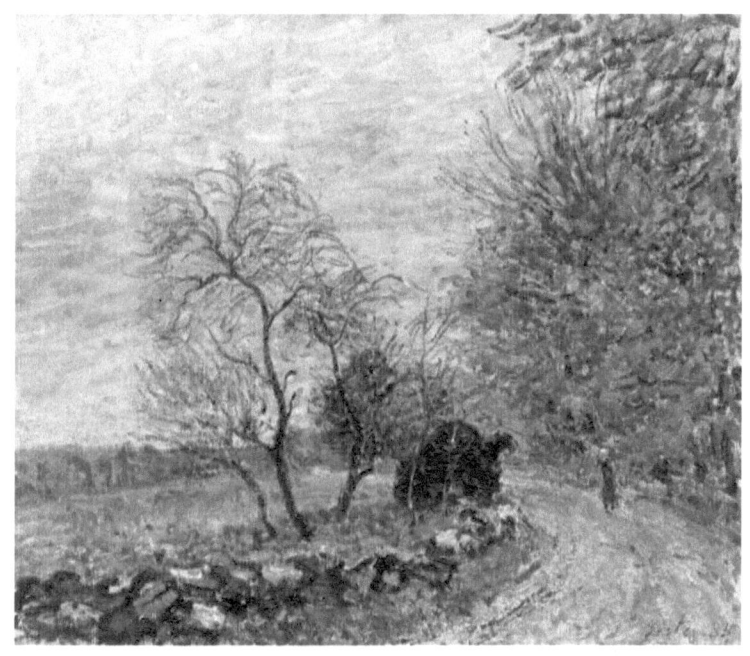

Along the woods in Autumn
1885, oil on canvas

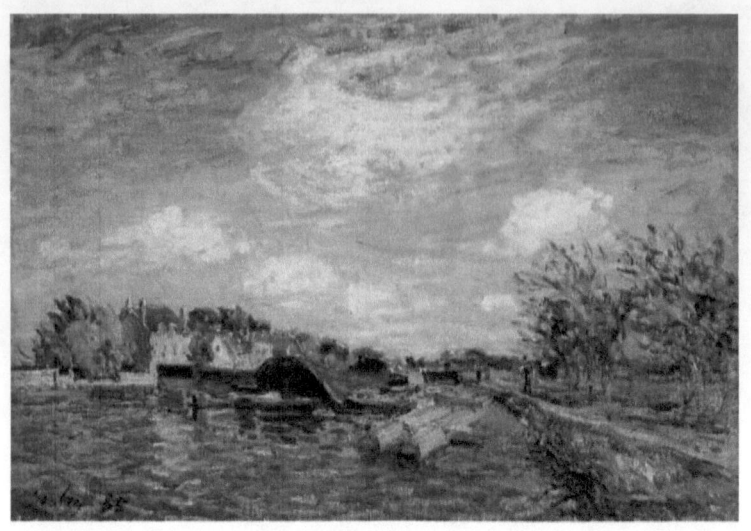

By the Loing
1885, oil on canvas

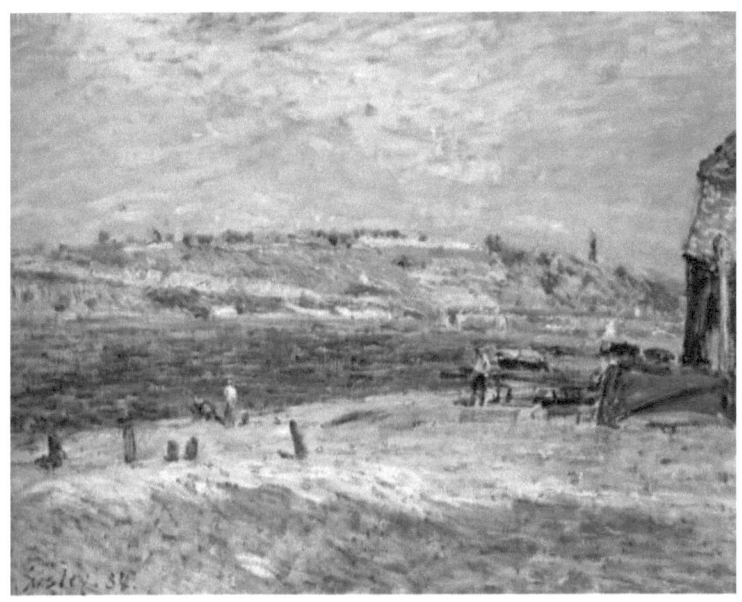

The River Bank at Saint-Mammes
1885, Oil on canvas,

Almost without striving for the effects of airiness,
transience, and translucency made fashionable by the
Impressionists, without concerning himself about a
specific subject, Sisley juxtaposes dense, resonant
colours. In so doing, he constructs a bridge to the
decorativeness of Pierre Bonnard and Edouard
Vuillard.

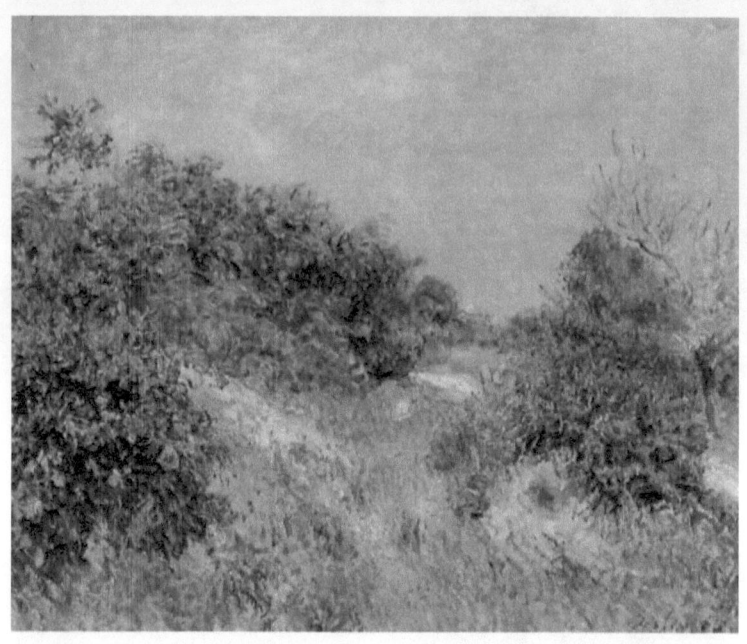

Edge of Fountainbleau Forest - June Morning
1885, oil on canvas

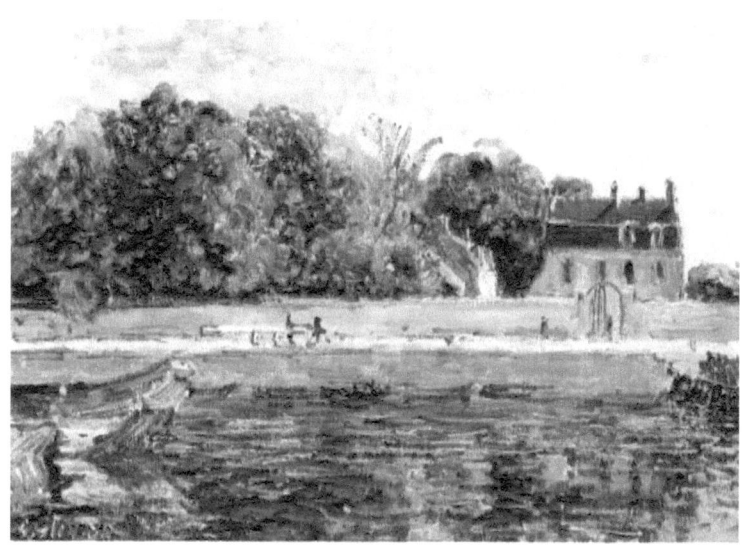

Saint-Mammes - House on the Canal du Loing
1885, oil on canvas

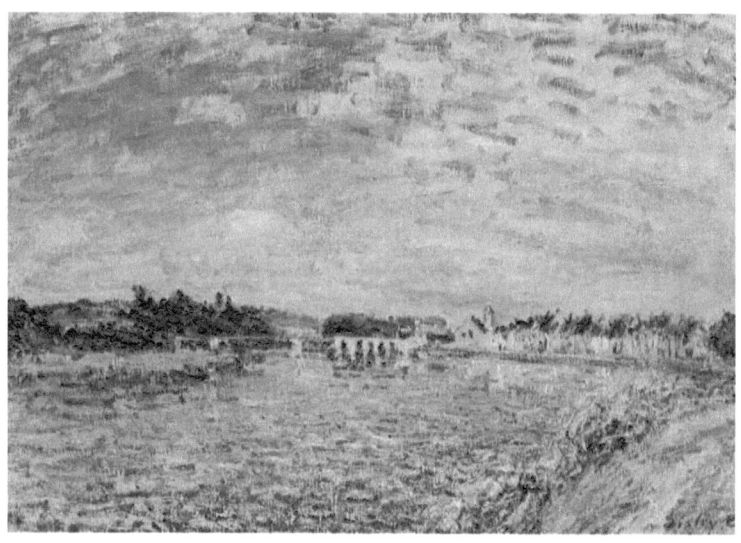

Saint-Mammes – Evening
1885, oil on canvas

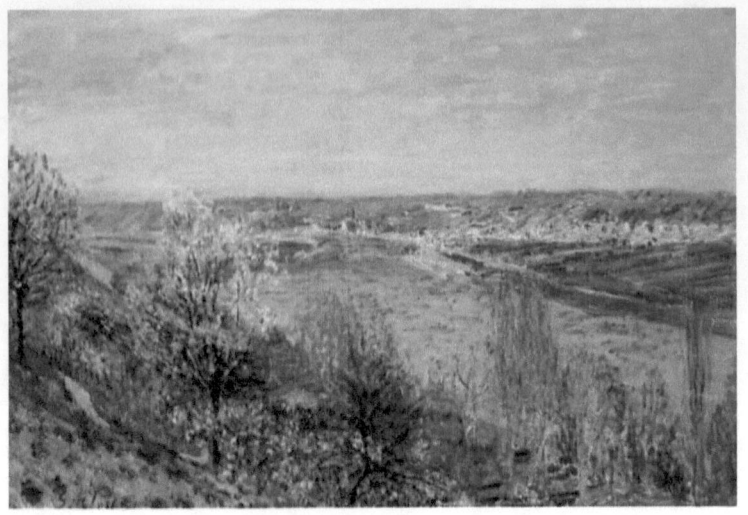

Village of Champagne at Sunset – April
1885, oil on canvas

The scene was painted from a spot at the edge of the Forest of Fontainebleau near Les Sablons, a modest hamlet where Sisley lived from 1883 until 1886. Standing on a steep rise above the plain of Veneux, Sisley looked northeast across the Seine toward the village of Champagne. In 1880, shortly after his arrival in the region, Sisley had painted Champagne at closer range, positioning himself directly across the river near the hamlet of By. These earlier views, however, are conspicuously social images, depicting washerwomen at the water's edge and the path leading to the embarkation point of the old ferry to Champagne, which had gone out of use in 1872. The present painting, in contrast, is a vision of romantic, almost audacious solitude, the humming life of the quays too far below to discern and the buildings of Champagne a mere stippling in the distance.

Indeed, the main pictorial drama of the painting stems from its tension between near and far, between the rich, variegated surface and the powerful suggestion of recession.

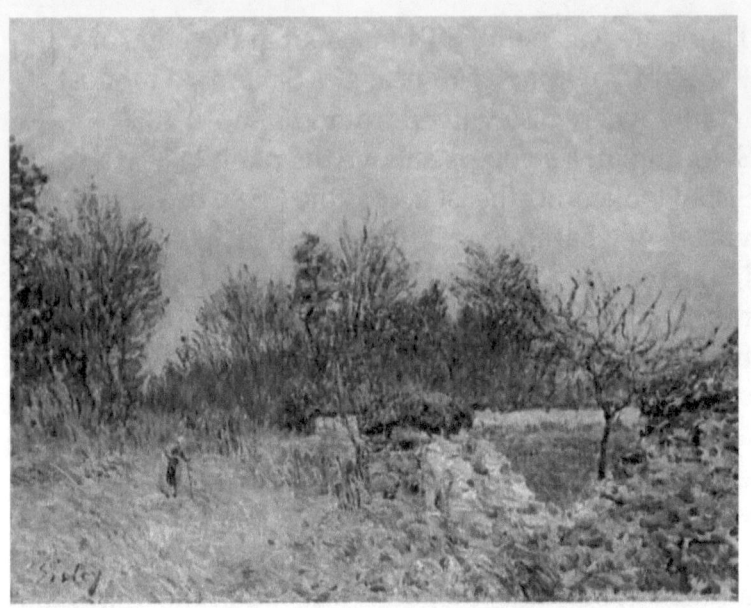

Edge of the Forest, December
1886, oil on canvas

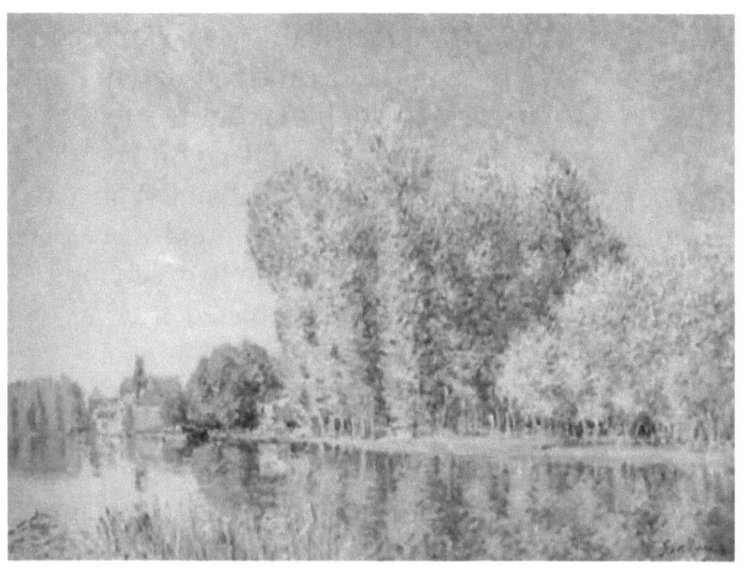

Le Loing à Moret
1886, oil on canvas

During the second half of the 1880s, Sisley explored through painting in series landscape at different times of the day and seasons, one of his favourite subjects being the town of Moret, as viewed from different vantage points along the river Loing. Painted on a magnificent summer afternoon, the present work is a superb exploration of the relationship between land, water and sky. The town itself is depicted at some distance to the left, on the opposite bank to which Sisley has taken his vantage point, successfully achieving a sense of depth and space. Discernable are the Provencher watermill, the church, and the twelfth-century town gateway, the Porte du Bourgogne. But the architectural elements of the painting give way to the bank on the right dominated by a proud row of poplars, their sun-gilt crowns massed against and almost cloudless vivid blue sky. Town, sky and lush greenery are all reflected in the calm surface of Le Loing, a celebration of vivid colour and pure and intense light.

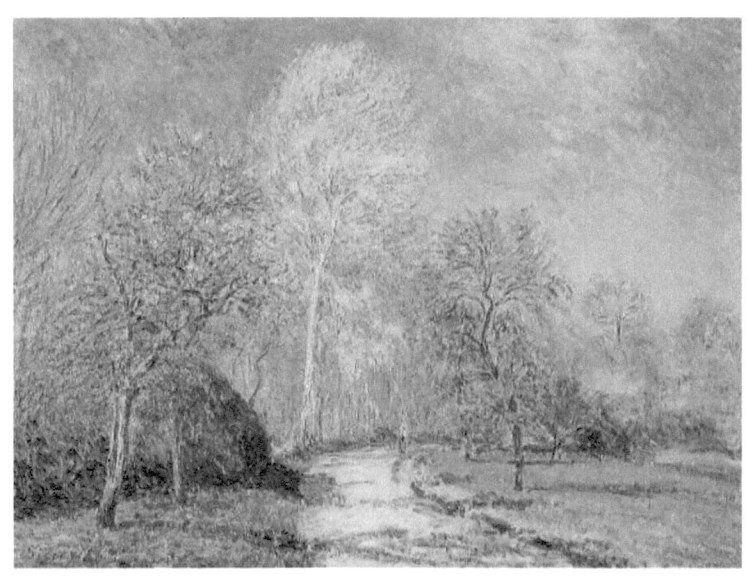

A May Morning in Moret
1886, oil on canvas

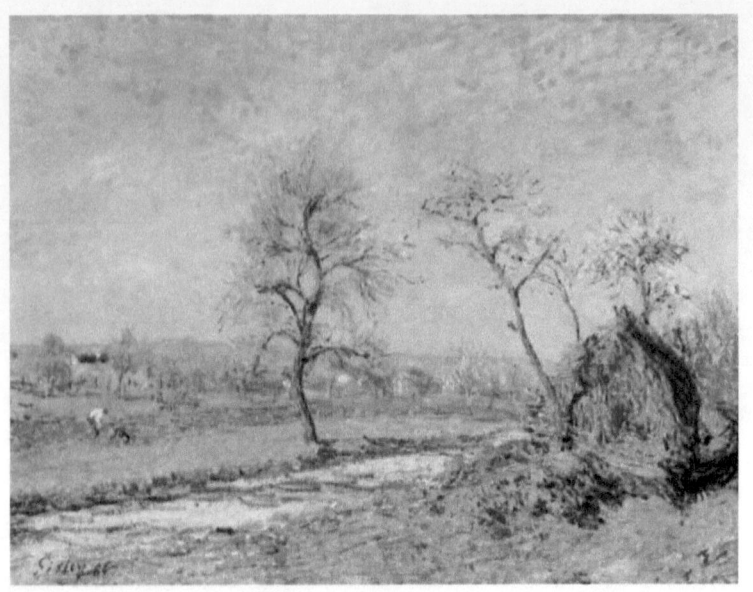

Road at Veneux
1886, oil on canvas

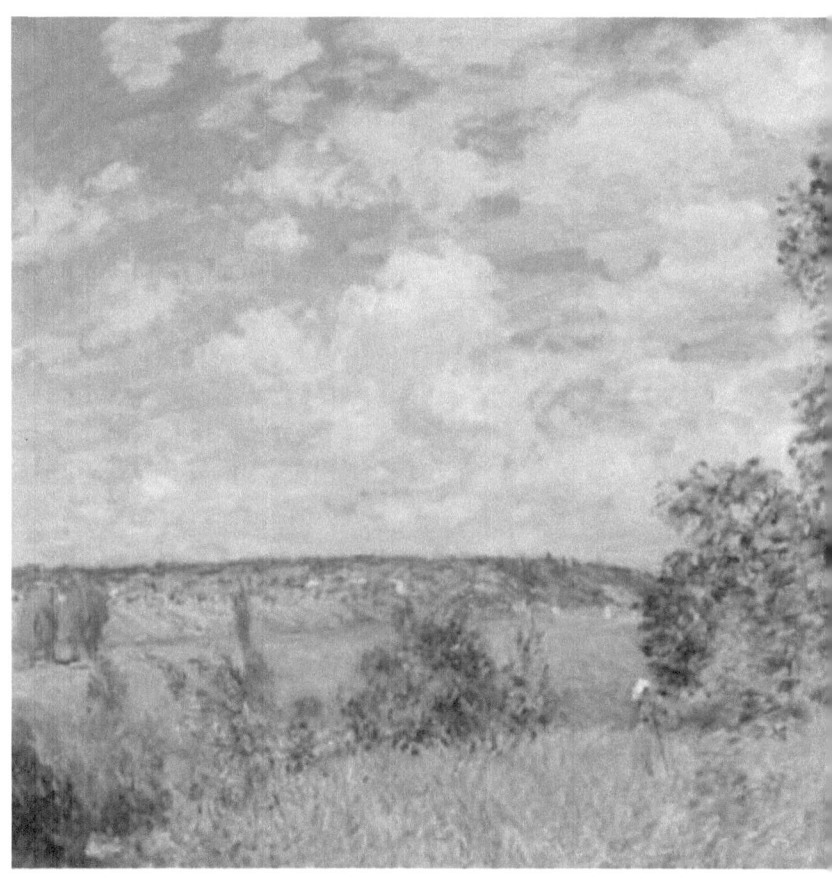

Haymaking - Afternoon in June
1887, oil on canvas

The present canvas is unusual in Sisley's work from this period for its elevated vantage point and panoramic sweep. Rather than setting up his easel at the water's edge, as he so often did, Sisley has selected a spot in a grassy field on higher ground, looking down toward the river. The edge of the meadow--the boundary between near and far--is delineated by a line of low shrubs and, at the far right, a cluster of tall trees. The latter are cropped by the upper edge of the canvas, emphasizing their proximity to the viewer. A single figure stands in the foreground, framed by an opening in the vegetation; his costume echoes the brilliant blue of the distant hills and the high summer sky. The middle ground of the composition, beyond the meadow's edge, is structured in a series of horizontal bands: a low grassy plain, the narrow blue ribbon of the river, the gentle slope of the hills beyond.

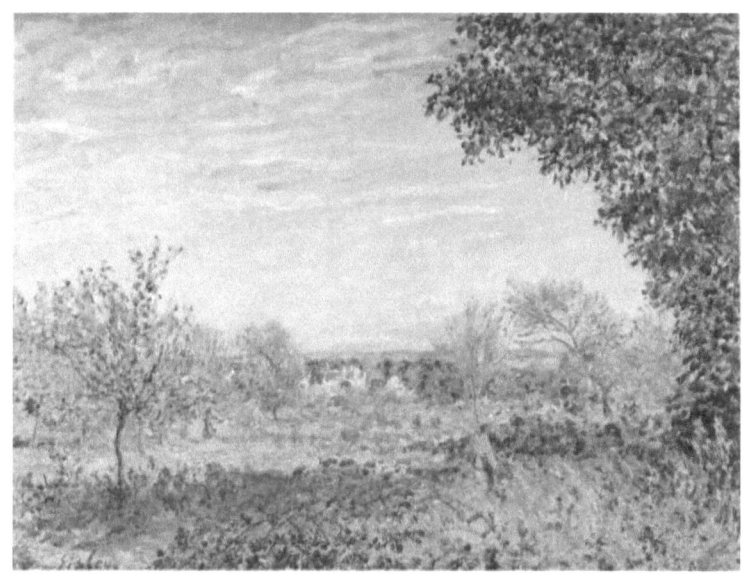

September Morning
1887, oil on canvas

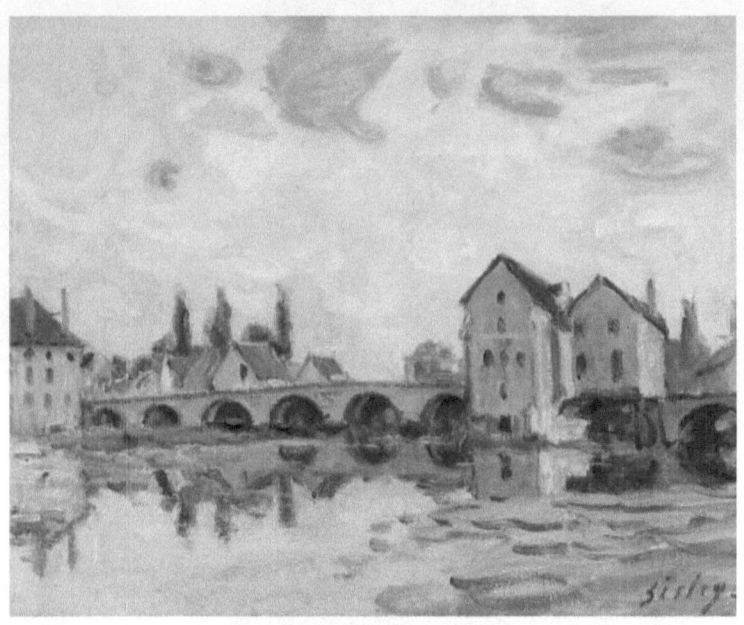

Moret sur Loing
1887, oil on canvas

Painted in 1887, just a year before Sisley settled
permanently in the charming medieval town of Moret-
sur-Loing for the last decade of his life, this rendering
of the Pont de Moret was amongst the first he painted
of this preferred motif.

Approximately forty miles southeast of Paris, near Fontainbleau, Moret-sur-Loing, with its particular historic charm and natural beauty, perfectly fit the mold of the artist's ideal subject matter. In the present lot, Sisley depicts Moret-sur-Loing, as seen from the opposite bank of the Loing River in the early hours of the day. With painterly, confident brushstrokes the artist perfectly captures the purple hues of morning light and the fragmented reflections across the dappled surface of water. The iconic architectural arches of the bridge which link the town centre with the road to Saint-Mamms dominate the composition, dividing the canvas between the expanse of sky above and the river in the foreground. Not unlike his artistic counter-parts, Sisley demonstrated his enthusiasm for the subject by painting it repeatedly en plein air from various vantages along the river bank, at any time of day, and in various seasons. The paintings which Sisley created in Moret-sur-Loing are often thought to be his most assured, as he explored the various light effects on this idyllic stretch of the Loing River.

While the Pont de Moret remained Sisley's chosen motif at the end of his life, he would also focus an entire series of works on the church of this small town, the Église de Notre-Dame, in 1893-1894. In 1899, when the artist died, the populace of Moret-sur-Loing sought to raise a monument in honour of the artist who so often celebrated their town in his paintings.

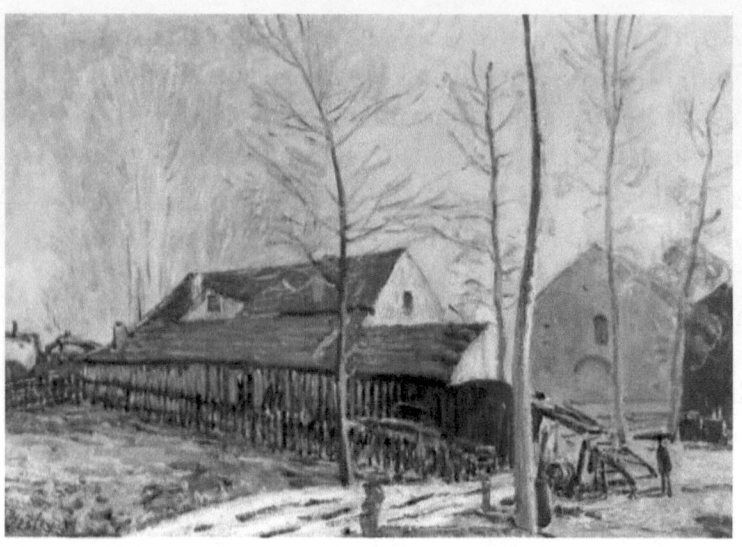

The Mills of Moret, Frost, Evening Effect
1888, oil on canvas

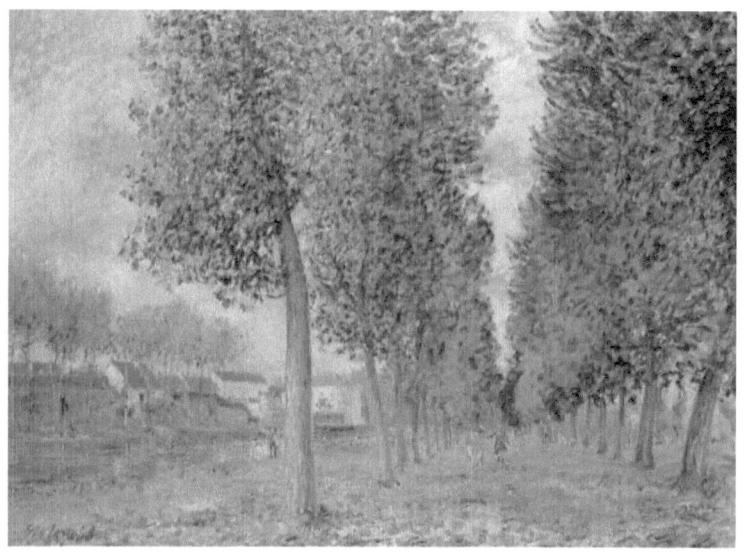

The Poplar Avenue at Moret, Cloudy Day, Morning
1888, oil on canvas

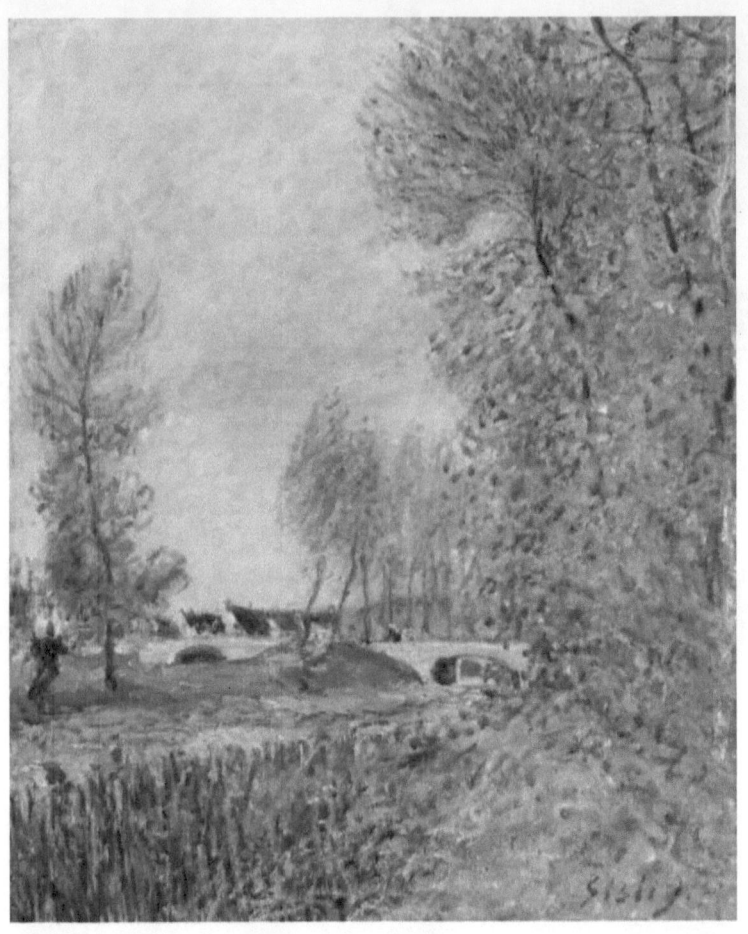

Bridge of the Orvanne
1888, oil on canvas

This picture appears to be a rare early example of a view of the Orvanne, a small tributary to the Moret. This was a tributary which joined the Seine near Morey-sur-Loing, where Sisley spent a great deal of his life and created some of his most celebrated landscapes.

Sisley has selected a composition that combines the rhythmic vertical punctuation of the trees, including those which appear to frame the image on the right, with the looping horizontal form of the bridge and the flickering streak of blue of the water itself. Dominant above all this is the sky.

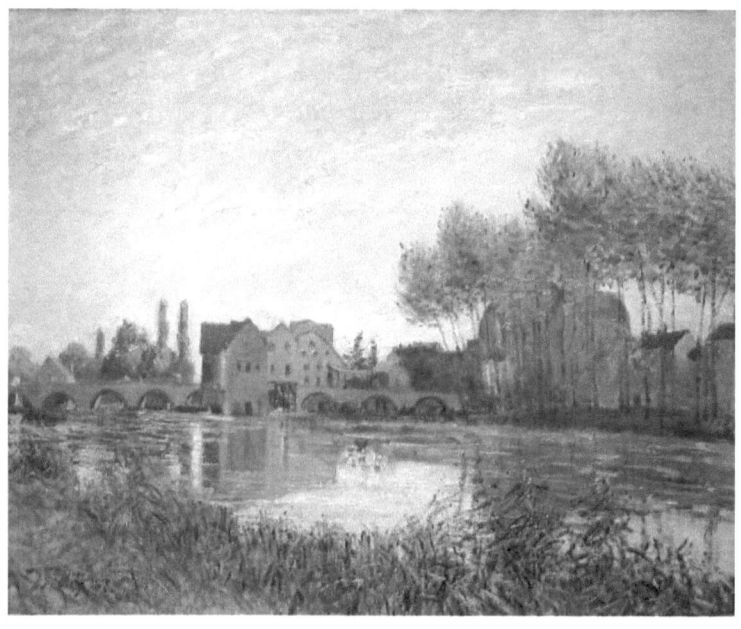

Sunset at Moret
1888, oil on canvas

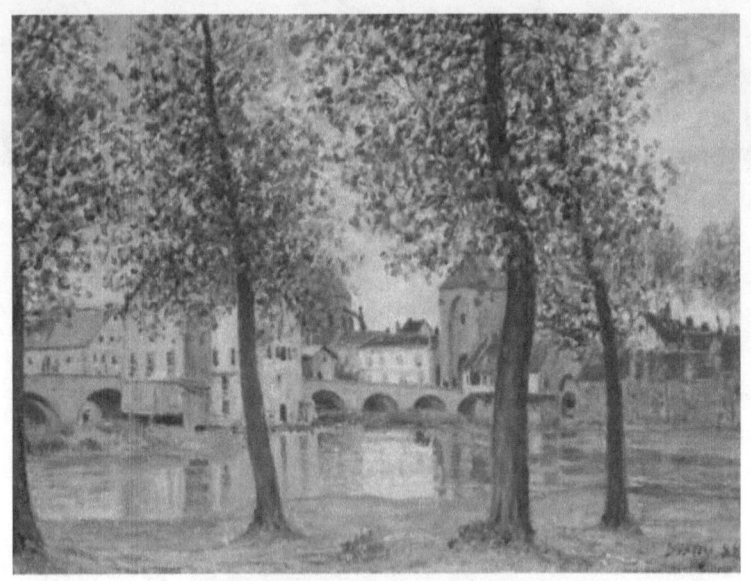

Bridge at Moret-sur-Loing
1888, Oil on canvas

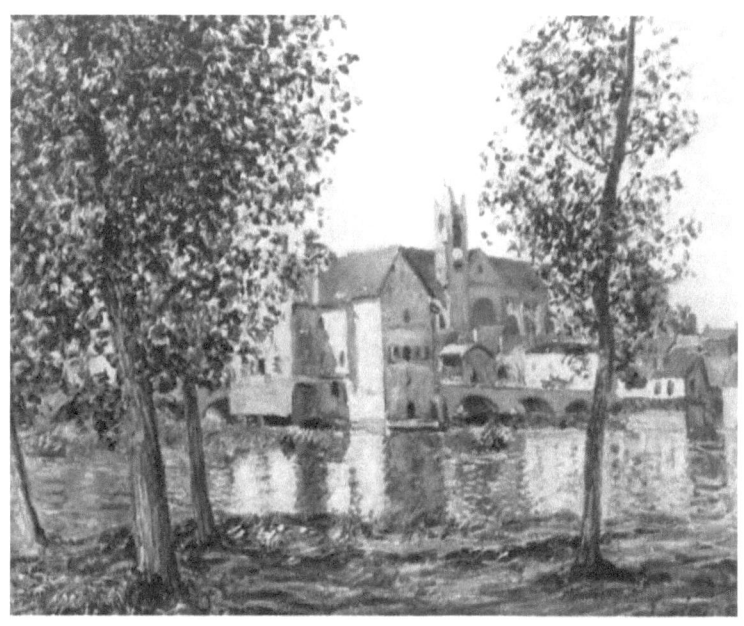

Moret-sur-Loing in Morning Sun
1888, Oil on canvas

Sisley went tirelessly in search of motifs along the Seine
and its tributaries, he looked no further. He abided by
views of village streets, or of interesting groups of
buildings, he would be drawn to an old stone bridge,
the kind of subject that had fascinated painters since
Corot. In unprepossessing patches of gardens or
meadows, landscapes on the skirts of towns or along
river banks, he could often discover the most arresting
colour or light effects.

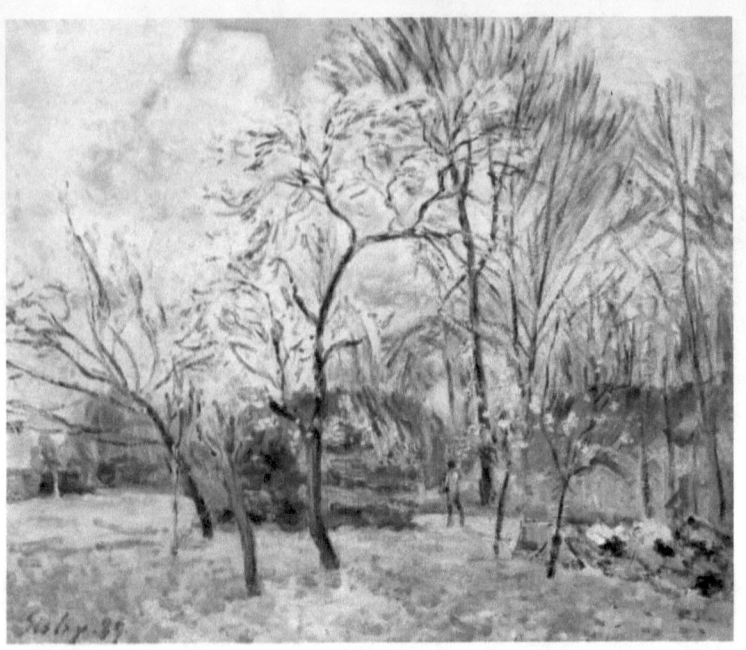

The First Day of Spring
1889, oil on canvas

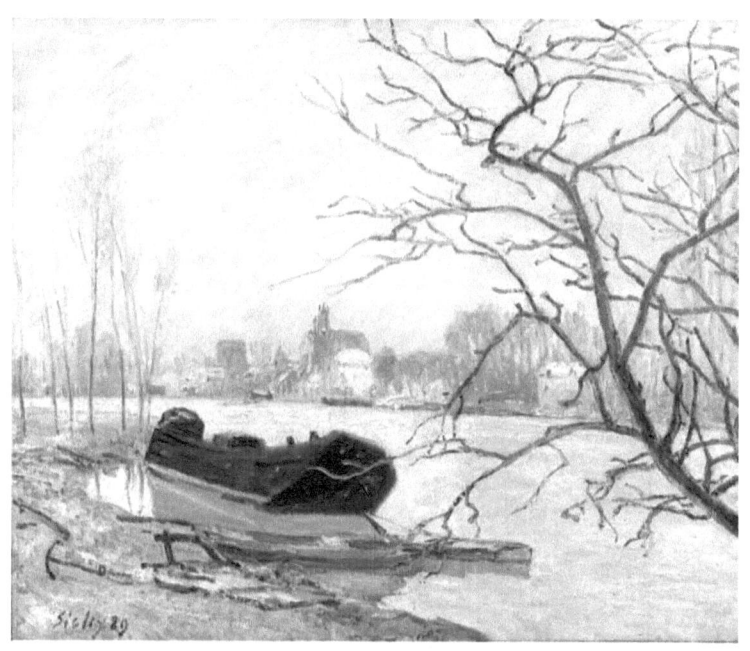

The Loing at High Water
1889, oil on canvas

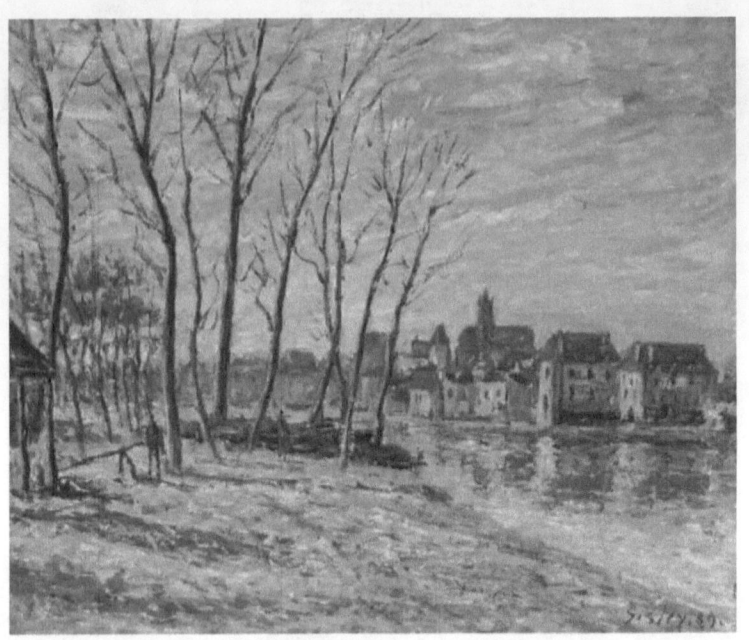

Vue de Moret
1889, oil on canvas

Painted in 1889, Vue de Moret dates from the year of
Sisley's return to the titular town on the River Loing,
near Fontainebleau. Sisley had moved to Moret-sur-
Loing originally at the beginning of the decade, but had
then left it, living in other towns in the vicinity, making
sure that he was never too far away and that he was
therefore still able to capture the many viewpoints that
it offered, be it the church, the watermills, the bridge or,
as here, the boatyard a little downstream from the
settlement. The scene in Vue de Moret was clearly one
that appealed to Sisley, as he painted it several times,
firstly in a group of pictures from the previous year and
then again in another work now in the Yale University
Art Gallery. There is an engaging human content in the
figures in the foreground, adding a contrast with the
more distant houses and other buildings in the
background.

While Sisley had deliberately maintained his proximity
to Moret, allowing him to paint it again and again from
his nearby homes, his return in November 1889
allowed him to tackle the subjects all the more easily.
The lack of foliage on the trees in Vue de Moret implies
that this picture may well date from this period of
return. The picture is suffused with the pinks of the
rising sun, casting their shadows in the trees, allowing
Sisley to explore the fleeting vision and fleeting
sensations that made him such a celebrated
Impressionist, especially amongst his peers. Henri
Matisse, for example, was moved to state that, 'A
Cézanne is a moment of the artist while a Sisley is a
moment of nature'

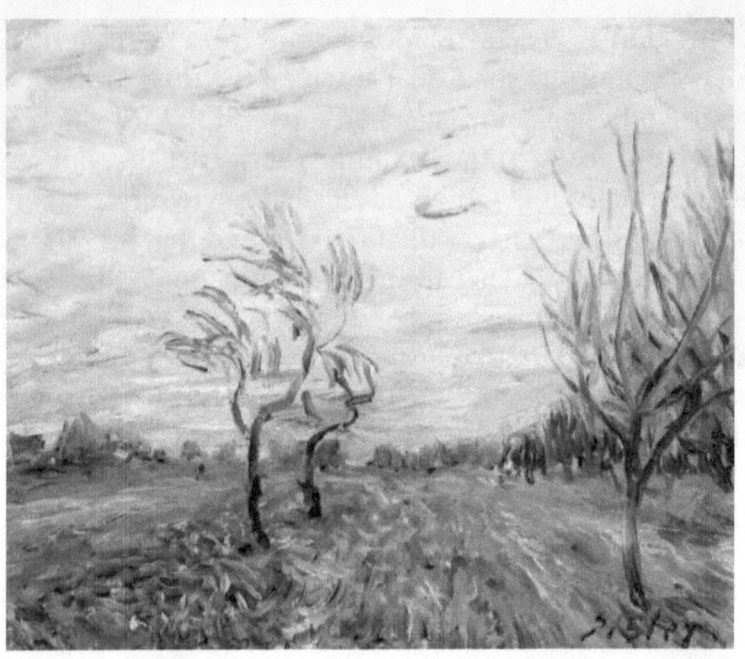

Orchard near Moret-sur-Loing
1890, oil on canvas

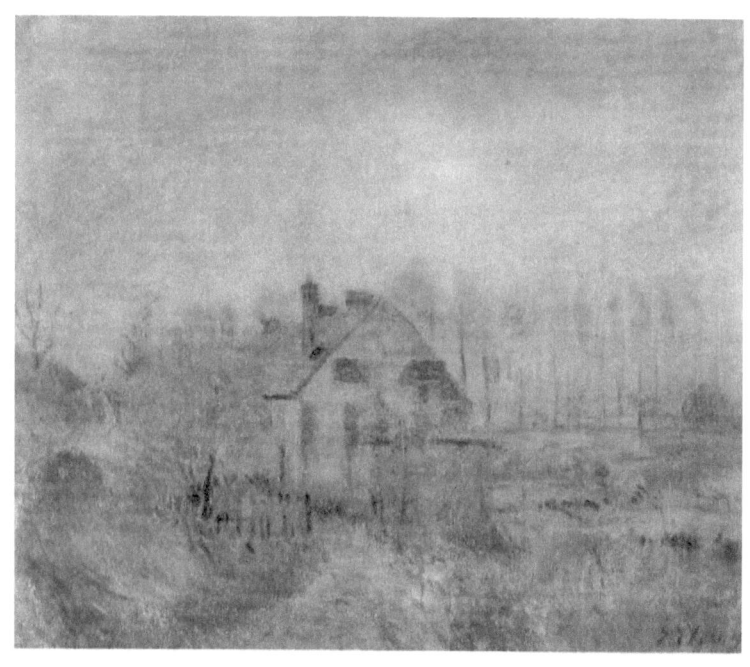

Springtime Scene – Morning
1890, oil on canvas

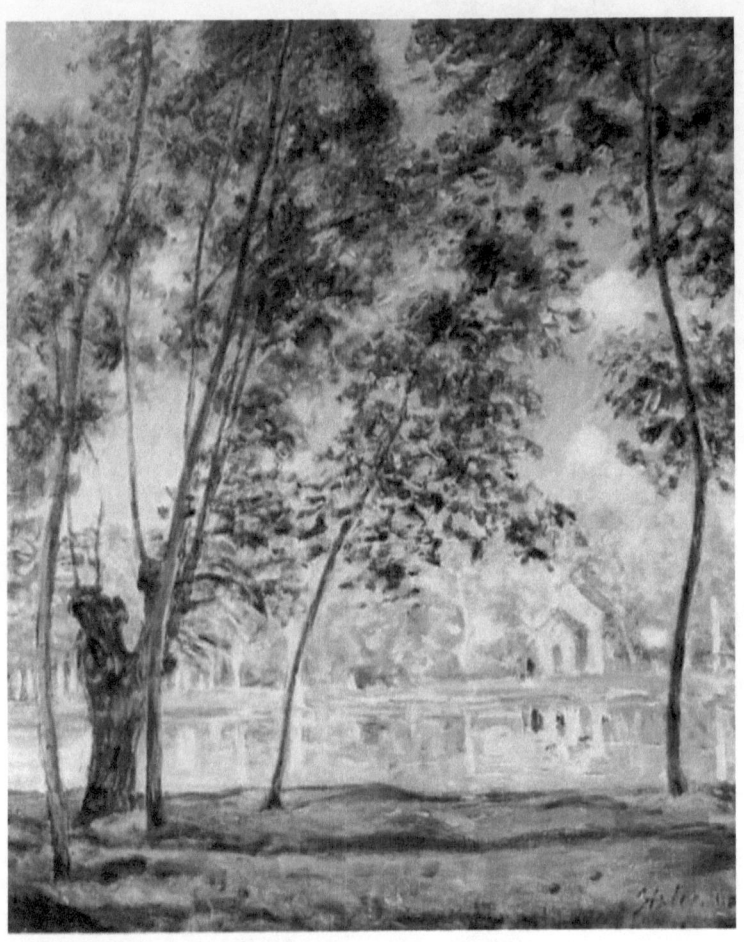

Sunny Afternoon - Willows by the Loing
1890, oil on canvas

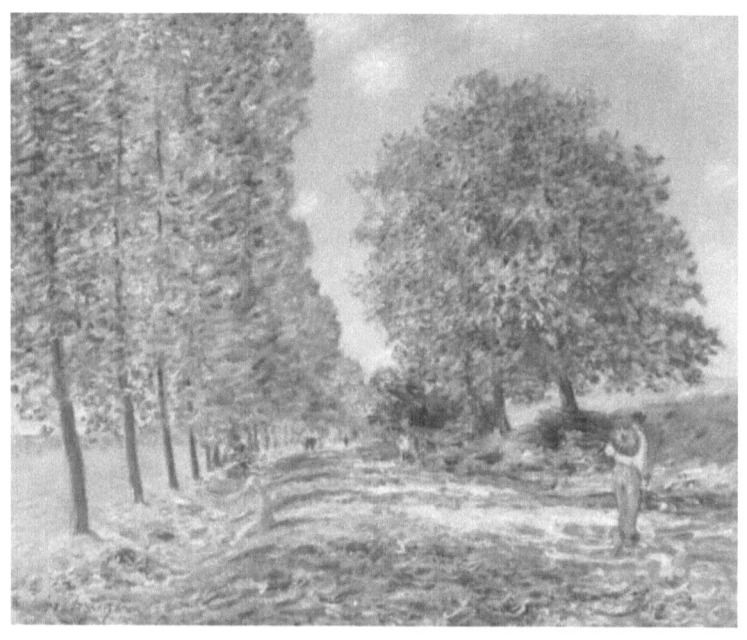

The avenue of poplars along the Loing Moret
1890, oil on canvas

In the present painting, Sisley has set up his easel on one of the paths along the riverbank near Moret, with a stately allée of poplars on the left and the Loing just barely visible in the distance through the screen of trees. There is no sign of the town center itself, however, suggesting that we may be standing on the right bank of the Loing looking downstream, away from Moret; on the opposite side of the river would be the wash-house that Sisley painted on several occasions. The receding diagonals of the path, punctuated by the evenly spaced, rigorously vertical tree trunks, lead the eye gently into depth, while the towering height of the poplars, extending even beyond the upper edge of the canvas, counters Sisley's characteristically low horizon line. The highly structured composition is balanced by the freshness of the execution, particularly in the free play of leaves against the summer sky and the dappled pools of white light that spill onto the grassy path.

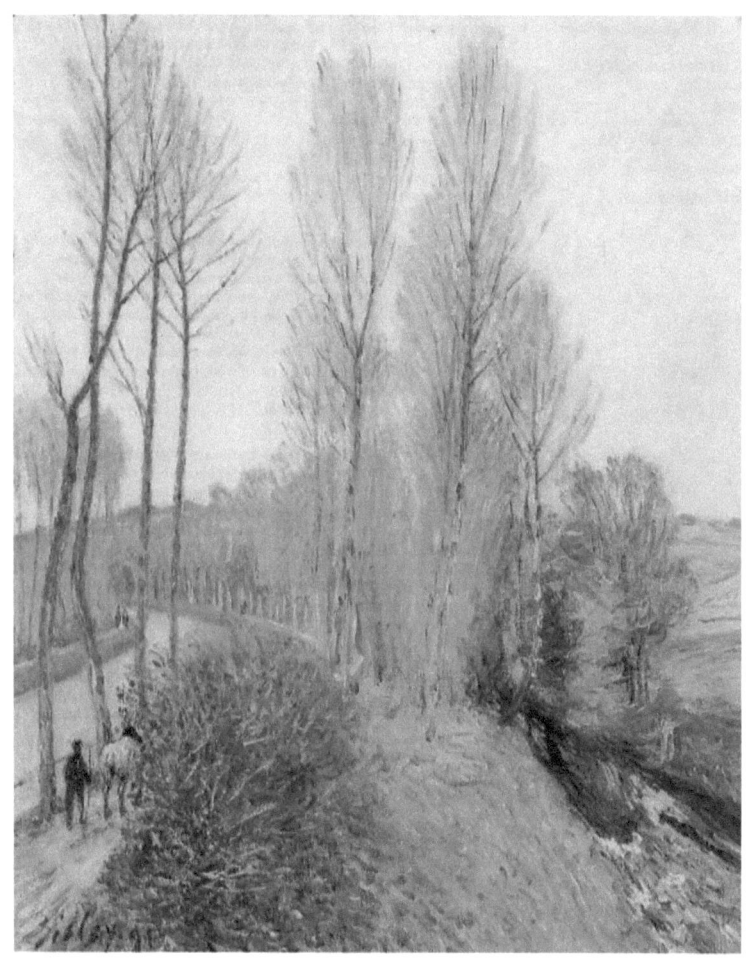

Path along the Loing Canal
1891, oil on canvas

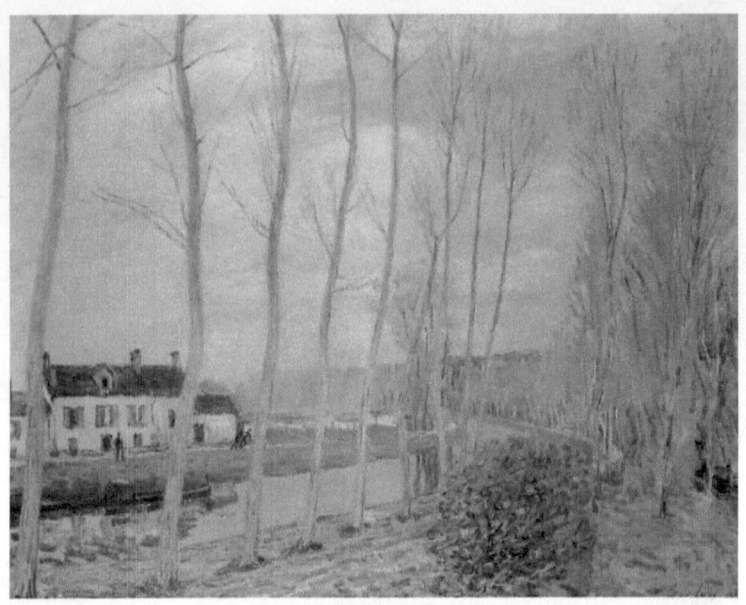

The Loing Canal at Moret
1892, oil on canvas

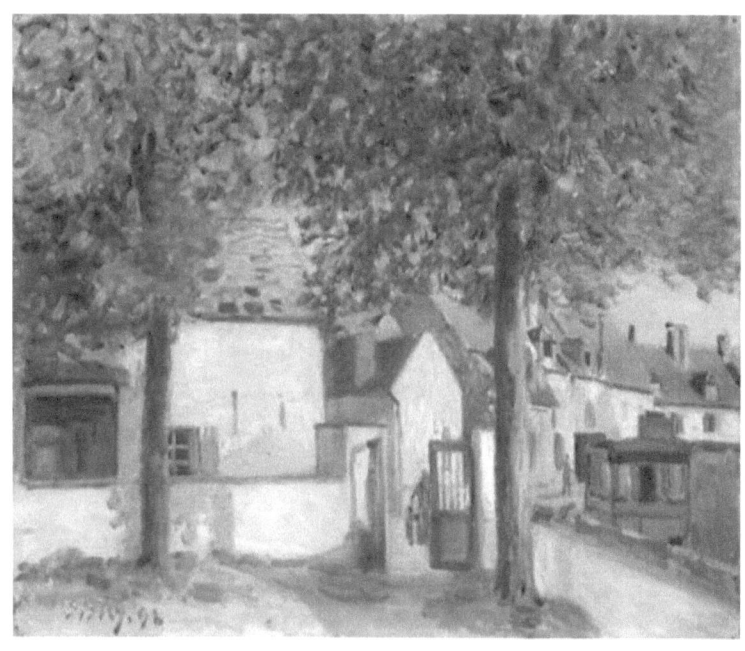

View in Moret (Rue de Fosses)
1892, oil on canvas

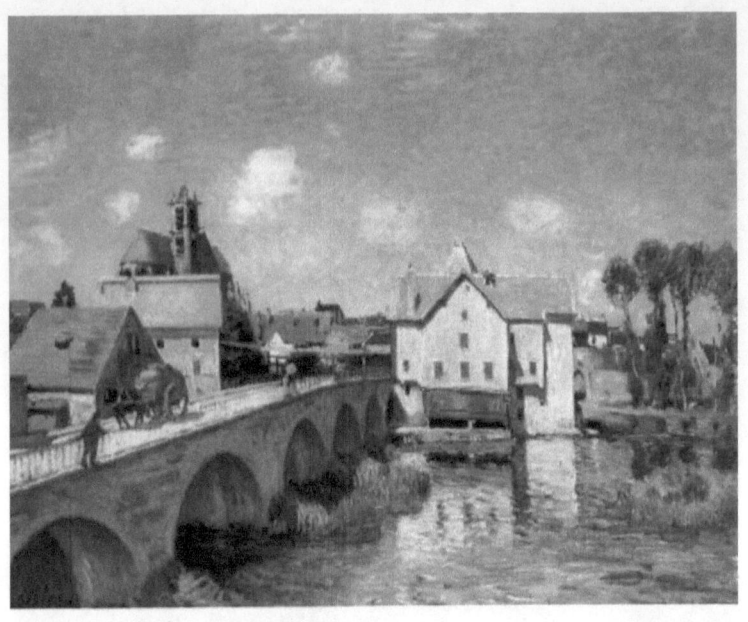

The Bridge at Moret
1893, Oil on canvas,

Sisley went tirelessly in search of motifs along the Seine
and its tributaries, he looked no further. He abided by
views of village streets, or of interesting groups of
buildings, he would be drawn to an old stone bridge,
the kind of subject that had fascinated painters since
Corot. In unprepossessing patches of gardens or
meadows, landscapes on the skirts of towns or along
river banks, he could often discover the most arresting
colour or light effects.

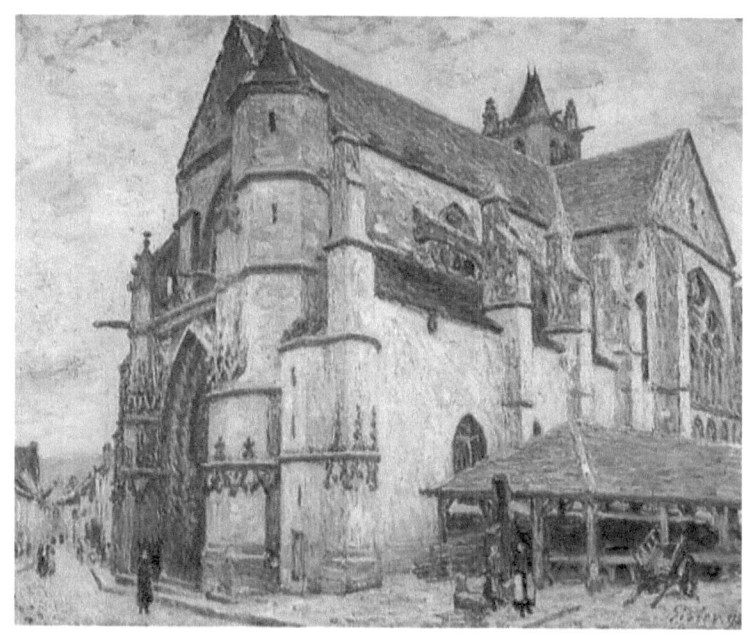

The Church at Moret, Icy Weather
1893, oil on canvas

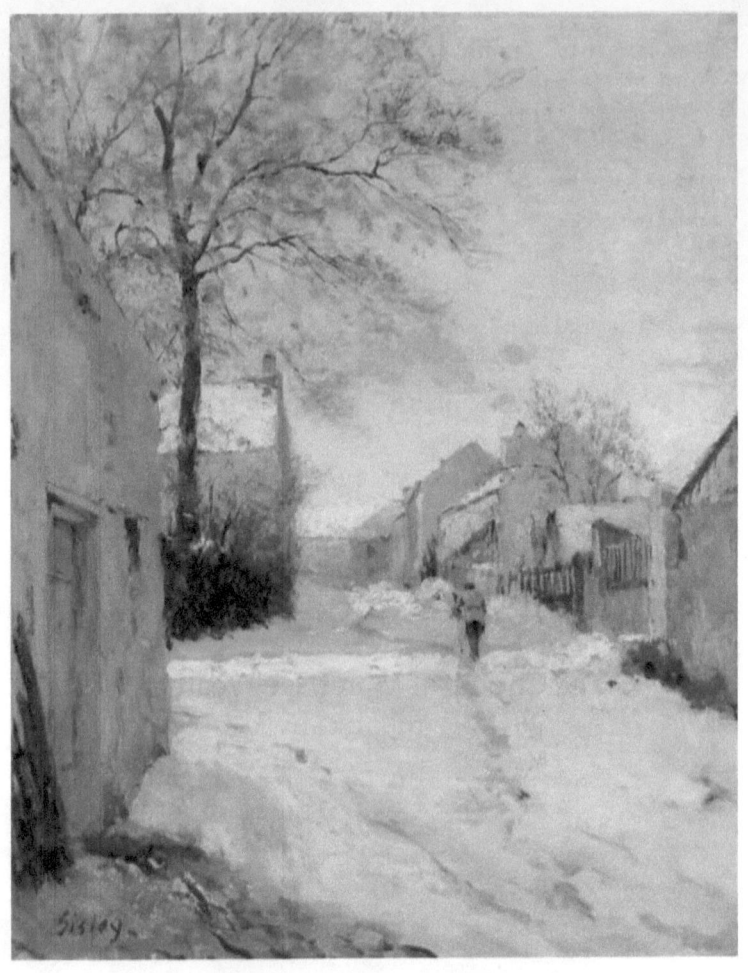

A Village Street in Winter
1893, oil on canvas

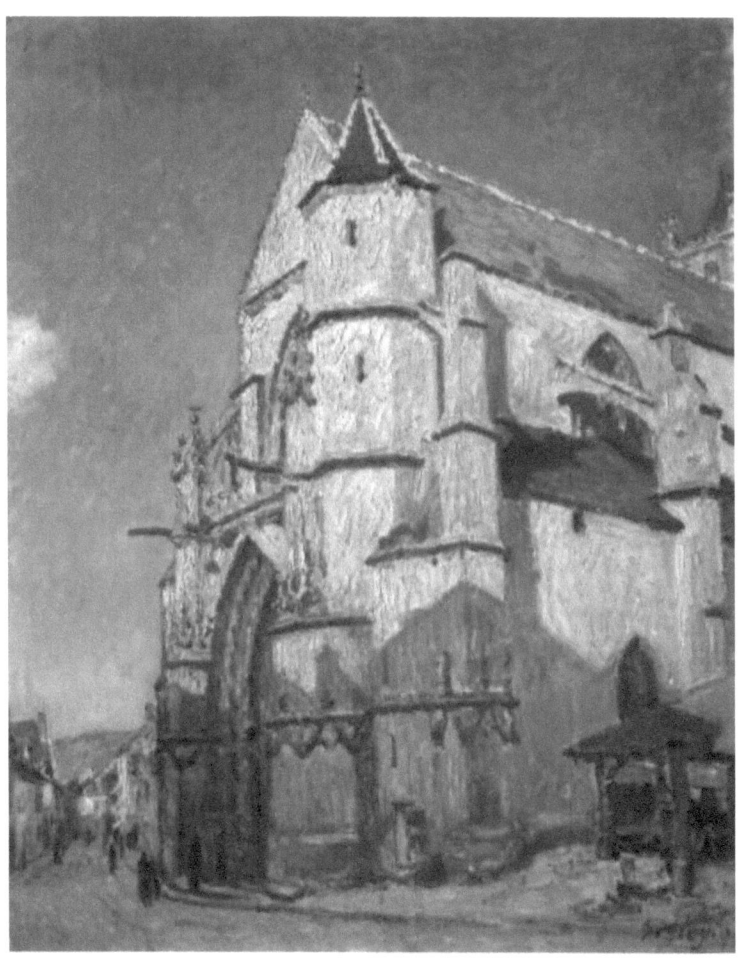

The Church at Moret, Evening
1894, Oil on canvas

Sisley's motifs and view of Nature placed him too plainly as an emulator of Monet, and he had no material distinctly his own that could have asserted his own individuality. This became most apparent when in 1893-94, parallel to Monet's Rouen cathedral series; he painted about 15 views of the church at Moret. Like all Sisley's later works, they are firmly painted, and evidently aim to give a rather ordinary sense of the appearance of the building instead of the veils of light and colour impressions Monet registered when looking at his cathedral. Sisley's work focussed on the thing seen, but art was evolving towards a more subjective emphasis on configurations of colours and shapes.

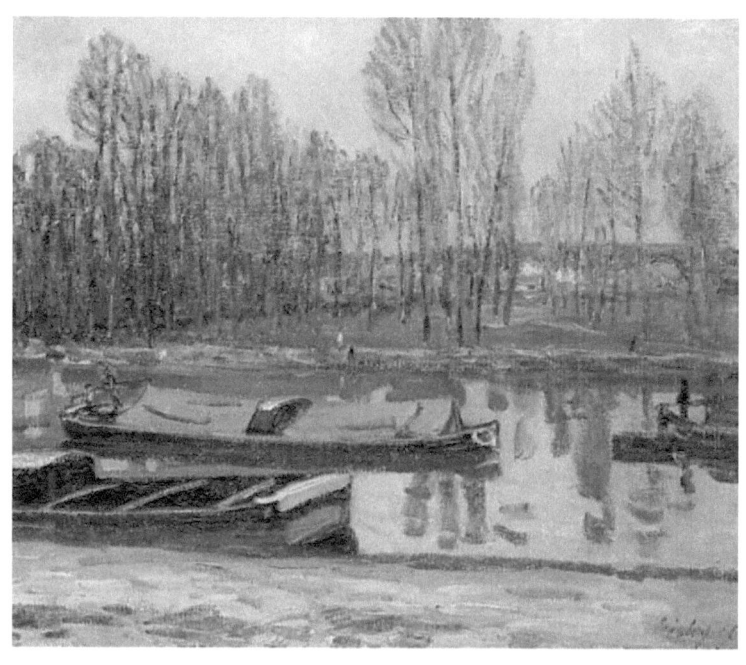

Barges on the Loing Canal, Spring
1896, oil on canvas

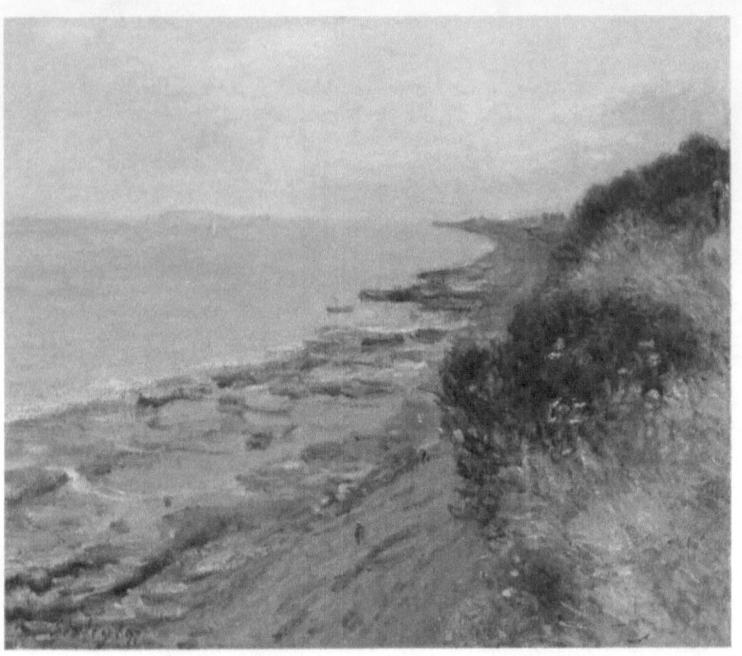

Cliffs at Penarth, Evening, Low Tide
1897, oil on canvas

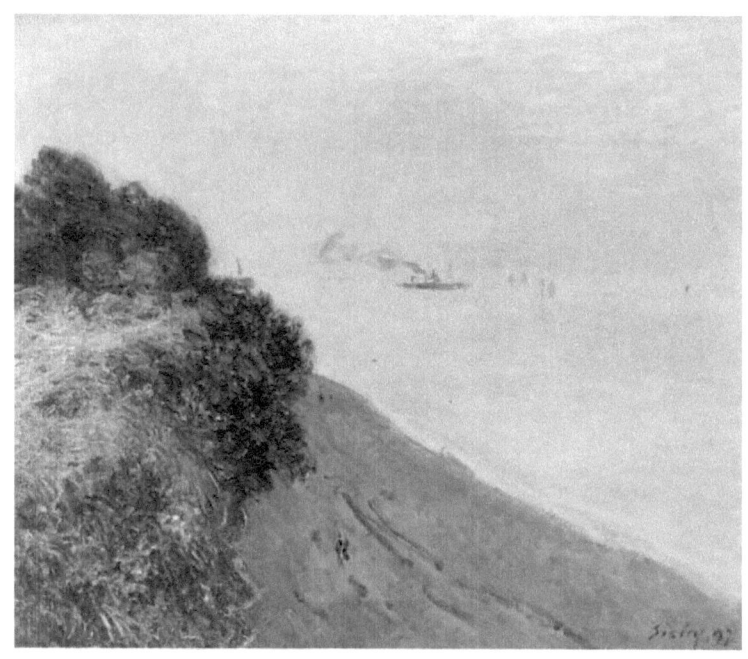

The English Coast, Penarth
1897, oil on canvas

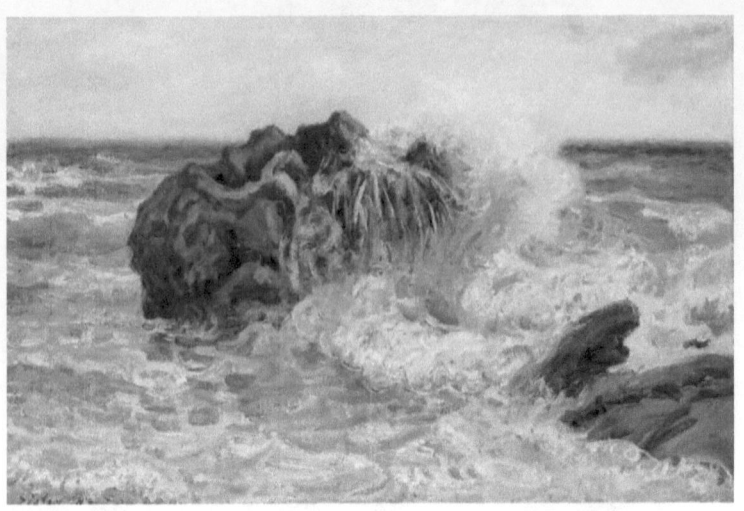

La vague, Baie de Langland (Pays de Galles)
1897, oil on canvas

This painting is a powerful exploration of the effect of light on the sea as white-tipped wave's crash on a solid mass of rock. The coastal scenes painted by the Anglo-French Impressionist in Wales are the only seascapes in his oeuvre, and recall the atmospheric views of the Breton coast painted in 1886 by his friend Monet at Belle-Île-en-Mer. It was at the suggestion of one of Sisley's most significant patrons of the 1880s and 1890s, François Depeaux, that the artist spent the summer months from July to September of 1897 in Penarth, near Cardiff and at Langland Bay, a few miles from Swansea on the Gower Peninsula.

Not only a period of significant creative fulfillment, Sisley's visit to Wales was also one of great personal importance as, on 5 August 1897 in Cardiff, he finally married his longtime companion, Eugénie Lescouezec after over thirty years of living together. They spent what was effectively their honeymoon at the Osborne Hotel on the edge of a cliff at Langland Bay overlooking Lady's Cove and the subject of the present painting.

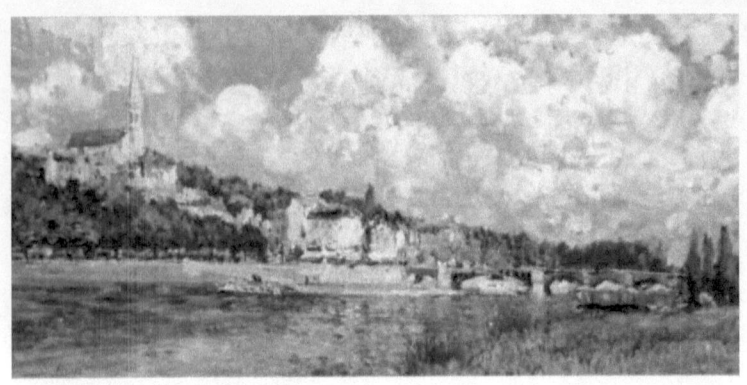

The River at Saint Cloud
N.d., oil on canvas

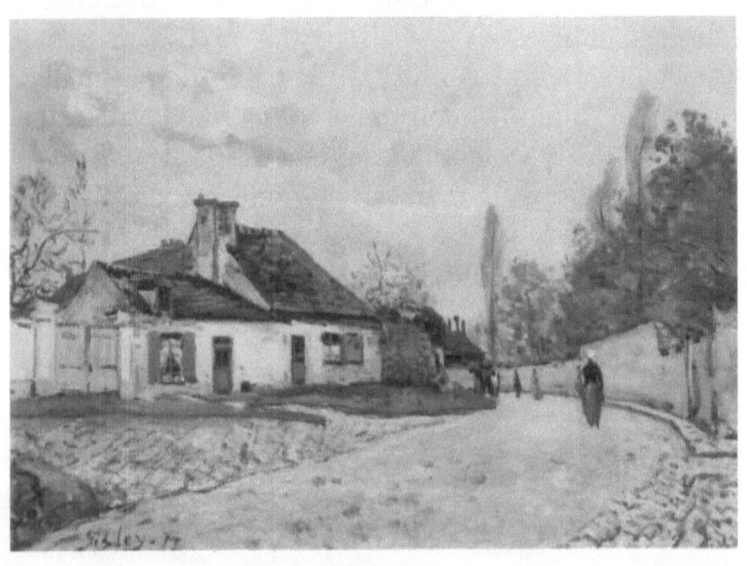

Voisins Street in Louveciennes
N.d., oil on canvas